Making Sound Money Moves

Financial Playbook for All Jocks

43 Reasons Professional Athletes Have Jacked-Up
Financial Lives and What *You* Can Learn from
Their Foul Plays

Lynda Paul, CFP®, CPA, MBA
Certified Financial Planner™
Your Money Coach

EDU013000
BUS050030

LyndaPaul.com

In association with:
Elite Online Publishing
63 East 11400 South Suite #230
Sandy, UT 84070
www.EliteOnlinePublishing.com

ISBN: 979-8-9854414-0-6 (Hardback)
ISBN: 979-8-9854414-2-0 (Paperback)
ISBN: 979-8-9854414-1-3 (eBook)
ISBN: 979-8-9854414-3-7 (Audiobook)
ISBN: 979-8-9854414-4-4 (Hardback, no Jacket)

Cover Photo by Richard's Photography, San Antonio, Texas
Makeup by Joseph Cruz, San Antonio, Texas
Hair styled by Tanya Irvin, San Antonio, Texas
Copy Editor – Jodi Brandon, JodiBrandonEditorial.com
Book Designer – Goran Tovilovic

Printed in the United States of America

Share This Book

We all have a role to play in the financial literacy game.

Use this QR Code to purchase a book for a friend or purchase in bulk for a group of friends or an organization you have influence with.

For resources visit:
LyndaPaul.com

This book is about financial literacy and behavioral finance in honor of:

- National Mentoring Month (January)
- Financial Literacy Month (April)
- Mental Health Awareness Month (May)

One last disclaimer: While the book is heavy on financial behaviorism and psychological gobbledygook, I attest that I am not a psychologist, and I don't play one on TV. Views expressed are my own based on my personal observations, my mom experience, 35+ years in personal financial planning / corporate accounting, and searching the "Googles." Having raised three alpha males, one being an elite professional athlete, I know a little something-something about everything. Well, most things. Okay, some things.

Cliffton Jr, Brandon, and Darius

"The first mistake is, people say, 'Okay, I've got $11 million' [according to the contract]. You've got five [million dollars after taxes] over four years. So that million-dollar house that you thought you had $11 million, that you had $10 million more, that house then becomes more expensive. Most guys buy their mother a house or a car or something. They buy themselves a car. You've got a 2-to-4% agent fee. You got the NBA escrow. So that check gets eaten up."[1]

—Josh Childress, sixth pick of the 2004 NBA draft, who signed a four-year rookie contract worth $11.7 million

~~~~~~~~~~~~~~~~~~~

"I think there's a lot of players based on what I've seen, either mismanaged money or aren't in the position to make the right decisions financially because they're the first generation of wealth. It's hard to manage money when you've never had it before and everyone around you has never had it before."[2]

—CJ McCullum, 2015–2016 NBA League MVP

CONTENTS

A Note to Professional Athletes Around the World 13

Financial Literacy 101 17

FOREWORD 21

BACKDROP Pro Athletes' Career Perks and
the Sportin' Life Ecosystem 23

INTRODUCTION..27

CHAPTER 1 Dealing with Family and Friends 39

    Reason 1 Notoriously Loyal to a Fault 42

    Reason 2   Surrounded by Yes Men 47

    Reason 3 People Pleased...51

    Reason 4 Lifestyle Creep...53

    Reason 5 Meet the Barber, the Power Broker....................56

    Reason 6 Hiring Uncredentialed Family and Friends as
Professional Advisors 59

CHAPTER 2 Dealing with Professionals and Your Money 63

    Reason 7 Trust but Verify..65

    Reason 8 Million-Dollar Loans 67

    Reason 9   Do-it-All Sports Agent.....................................75

    Reason 10 The Vetting Game..78

    Reason 11 Just Answer 3 Questions, Please 81

    Reason 12 Background Checks..85

    Reason 13 Second Opinions 87

    Reason 14 Inexperienced Tax Preparers 89

    Reason 15 Sign Here, and Here, and Here 92

    Reason 16 Don't Ask Questions 97

    Reason 17 No Alias 100

Reason 18 No Budget and No Financial Accountability 104

Reason 19 What If? 109

Reason 20 The Need for a Comprehensive Financial Plan 115

CHAPTER 3 Dealing with Self and the Entrepreneurial Spirit 121

Reason 21 The Brain = Intellectual Capital 123

Reason 22 This Time It's Different 125

Reason 23 Merci Beaucoup 128

Reason 24 Emotional Immaturity 130

Reason 25 Instincts 133

Reason 26 The Power of Compound Interest: The Rule of 72 136

Reason 27 Creating Wealth 144

CHAPTER 4 The Entourage, Entertainment, Consumptive Behaviors, and Dopamine 149

Reason 28 The Personal Entourage: Everybody's Invited to the Party 154

Reason 29 *Big* Tip Energy 157

Reason 30 Turnt Up with Fam: VIP Bottle Service 162

Reason 31 Bruh, You Extra 166

CHAPTER 5 Physical and Mental Health 169

Reason 32 Ego 173

Reason 33 FOMO (Fear of Missing Out) 176

Reason 34 Imposter Syndrome 178

Reason 35 YOLO: Mavericks and Excessive Gambling 182

Reason 36 Making Mental Health an Afterthought 188

CHAPTER 6 Dealing with the Law, Including Tax Law 193

Reason 37 Catching Charges 196

Reason 38 State Domicile and Saving Tax Dollars 199

Reason 39 The Dreaded "Jock Tax" 202

CHAPTER 7 Groupies and Tinder Love 205

Reason 40 Baby Mama, Financial Drama 209

Reason 41 Divas and Financial Infidelity 215

CHAPTER 8 Paradigm Shift 217

  Reason 42 Victims: The Setup 224

  Reason 43 Frontloaded/Backloaded...............................228

RECAP 43 Reasons Professional Athletes Go Broke 235

CONCLUSION 239

ACKNOWLEDGMENTS & INSPIRATION 247

POSTSCRIPT 1 What Are Professional Sport Leagues and Player Associations Doing to Improve the Financial Literacy of Their Players? 251

POSTSCRIPT 2 The Race Card 255

POSTSCRIPT 3 Money Moves Savvy Millennials (Gen Yers) and Gen Zers Should Make Right Now 257

POSTSCRIPT 4 Collegiate Athletes and the Name Image Likeness (NIL) NCAA Rule Change 259

Enhancing Financial Literacy Among Student-Athletes Report..263

CHAPTER NOTES 267

ABOUT THE AUTHOR..283

Making money is one thing. Keeping money is another. Keep turning the pages to learn sound money habits so you'll never go broke.

Feed the Pig

A Note to Professional Athletes Around the World

Yes, you can have it all.

You've worked hard to get to this point. Persevered. Now you train and compete with the best, pushing through extreme physical and mental boundaries in an epic way. Game time, you leave everything on the field, court, track, or ice. Your passion for competition is undeniable. You are an elite performer who competes at the highest level and is regarded as a world-class athlete—the best of the best. You are paid good money to do what you love. You've got fame, a solid reputation, and a thriving personal brand. You are doing you on your terms. Here's the challenge: How can you keep what you've worked so hard to attain and live an amazing life now *and* during the second act, after you hang up your jersey?

"Having it all" is not a myth. It's possible. But since you have a limited window of opportunity to make good financial decisions, you need to make a commitment early in your professional career to adhere to sound money practices. This commitment includes spending way less than you earn and having the financial endgame in your thoughts at all times. You understand the assignment. Achieving your life's goals, living out your dreams, providing for your family in a spectacular way, acquiring things your heart desires, and attaining maximum success are all possible. And here's the best news: You get to decide what "all" is as you create a lifestyle and secure a living. You get to dictate which situations will work for you and which will not be acceptable. You're in a great position to have the power and freedom to create your own reality—the freedom to choose and pursue the life you desire. Many self-help gurus espouse you are the author of your existence. If this is true, and I believe it is, you—and only you—can define what success is, and only you can decide how best to attain it.

Is it selfish to think about yourself and your own future, before thinking about what would make others happy? Serving yourself and

13

MAKING SOUND MONEY MOVES

serving others are not mutually exclusive. You can do both. It is completely acceptable to want to reward yourself for your hard work—to enjoy the fruits of your labor. Go ahead and give yourself permission to enjoy your hard-earned prosperity. To *exhale*. What if self-care was the modern benign term for selfishness? Self-care, the practice of taking an active role in protecting your own well-being and happiness, is critically important. Self-care includes proper nutrition, stress-reduction exercises, and health and financial wellness; all are critically important to keep yourself happy and resilient. It's important you take good care of your mind, body, and soul every day, in every way. And your money too. As a pro athlete, practicing self-care isn't always easy. In a team setting you are asked to be self-less and do what's in the best interest of the team, the sport, and the community.

Your family and close friends are placing demands on your time and money, looking in most cases to benignly benefit from your hard work. Perhaps in their minds, these are harmless requests. But what's best for you? When we fly in an airplane, the flight crew reminds us, in the event of excessive turbulence and there is a drop in cabin pressure, that if we are traveling with a child or someone who requires assistance, we should secure our oxygen mask first, then assist the other person. Why? It is important to put on your mask first because, without oxygen, you might not be physically capable of assisting others. Is this an example of selfishness? The oxygen mask analogy is a great metaphor for self-care and for conducting your life—especially your financial life—in a self-preserving and most excellent way. Attending to yourself first ensures you will have the mental and physical facilities (resources) needed to take care of those who require assistance. Makes perfect sense.

Have you heard of the financial concept "pay yourself first"? Self-care, selfishness, self-preservation—whichever title you give it—is very important to maximize your economic viability. Do not feel the need to take care of everyone asking for financial assistance until you have properly secured your own financial future. How you feel about taking care of yourself and your money determines how you show up in relationships. You must be priority one, not in a selfish way but in a self-empowering way. Give yourself permission to take care of you and your future self, first! This book will help you uplevel your financial literacy skills and boost your confidence so you can secure a sound and successful financial future for yourself and your family.

What does financial success look and feel like? How should you go about setting goals? Attaining goals? Exceeding goals? How should you curate your personal brand? How much time and effort should you focus on your personal finances? Mental health? Who should you ask to help you create your financial game plan? Can you trust their advice? What kind of financial life do you want now? What about your future self? How do you think he wants to live after you retire from your current sports career? How does dating factor into your money management? Are you mindful about consensual sexual encounters? What is *sound* money management anyway? These are all personal questions that only you can successfully answer. The information contained in this book will help. Whether you desire to attain massive fame, epic wealth, master sound money-management concepts, or simply be the best financially literate person you can be, the good news is that you get to decide how. The opportunity to excel is yours.

This is a loosely scripted playbook to provide guidance to help you master your mental, physical, and financial game plan and to help create a sound money-management framework that will give you confidence to call your own shots. You've worked hard to arrive at this point. Doesn't it make sense to increase your intellectual capital, uplevel your financial literacy game, improve your financial decision-making, and achieve the financial success you deserve? What do you want your financial legacy to be? Only you can make it happen. Go. Be. Great!

> *"I can't tell you everything. But if you want to make history you gotta call your own shots."*[3]
>
> —LeBron James, Super Bowl LVI Commercial, February 13, 2022

Photo Credit: wallpaperset.com/lebron-james

LeBron James, 4-time NBA Finals MVP, 19-time NBA All-Star,
All-Time leading scorer in NBA history

Financial Literacy 101

According to the U.S. Treasury's Financial Literacy and Education Commission, financial literacy is the ability to use knowledge and skills to manage financial resources effectively for a lifetime of financial well-being.[4] Being financially literate helps you make informed decisions regarding the use of money and financial assets. It influences how you save, borrow, invest, and manage your financial affairs. I am sure you would agree that understanding the nuances of your financial reality is critically important, whether it's:

- ✓ Learning how a checking account or a debit card works,
- ✓ Budgeting income and expenses and managing your monthly cash flow,
- ✓ Applying for a credit card and understanding the credit terms,
- ✓ Buying a home and calculating your monthly mortgage payment,
- ✓ Comparing a home equity loan to a home equity line of credit,
- ✓ Purchasing or leasing a new car or buying a used car,
- ✓ Choosing the best way to save for your child(ren)'s education,
- ✓ Buying insurance,
- ✓ Deciding how much to contribute to your 401(k), or
- ✓ Evaluating investments and determining asset allocations.

Having a firm grasp of financial knowledge also helps when evaluating the future value of contract provisions, or if it is prudent to invest in a business opportunity. Financial literacy affects your capacity to grow your wealth, avoid dangerous debt levels, and mitigate financial risks, and it has significant implications on your lifestyle choices, now and in the future.

In this digital age, when everything is available almost instantaneously, online shopping allows for the potential of overspending and an overextension of credit, which can lead to an explosion of personal debt and an implosion of negative emotions, even depression. Lack of financial understanding is a major cause of personal stress and can lead to poor job performance and relationship issues in marriages or with significant others, which can exacerbate financial woes. According to research done by the National Financial Educators Council (NFEC), shortfalls in financial literacy cost Americans an estimated $352 billion dollars in 2021,[5] primarily from arcane banking and transaction fees, high-interest debt obligations, internet fraud, Ponzi schemes, and poor investment decisions (e.g., buying high and selling low instead of embracing the opposite time-tested investment philosophy of buying low and selling high). This amount may represent significant underestimates as many people who lack financial capability may not even be aware of their losses.

The financial cost of making poor money moves serves to demonstrate the importance of improving financial literacy to make sound financial decisions. Lacking financial knowledge can affect your personal financial situation in very powerful ways.

Eddie Johnson, who played 17 seasons in the NBA and is now a commentator for the Phoenix Suns and an author, gives this advice to young professional athletes in his book, *You Big Dummy: An Athlete's "Simple" Guide to a Successful Career:*[6]

1. Hire a team of financial advisors.
2. Pay your own bills. Do not delegate this very important business task.
3. Don't buy an abundance of toys, especially toys that depreciate.
4. Focus on kids' education.
5. Just learn to say *no*.

> *"The number one problem in today's generation and economy is the lack of financial literacy."*[7]
>
> —Alan Greenspan, former Chairman of the Federal Reserve (served 1987–2006)

Photo Credit: Spurs official release

NBA Rookie Year
Brandon Paul #3 San Antonio Spurs

FOREWORD

It's one thing to have aspirations, to have a passion and a specific goal. It's another thing to constantly speak it into existence and actually put in the work to see it to fruition. This book is the perfect example of this. All biases aside, I have not seen someone as passionate as my Mom has been about this book over the course of the last several years. The way she would speak about this, it made it seem almost as if I was writing the book myself! That is the amount of excitement I got just from hearing her speak on the content that will be shared with you all. Being a child of God, mother, wife, business owner, and lover of dance and music are just a few of the things this woman is seriously passionate about.

Her decades of experience in money management mixed with her personal relationship to the topic of financial literacy, having lived in a household with four former or current athletes (including two professionals), gives her a bit of an outsized advantage when it comes to having specific knowledge on the subject. This, added with her relentless search for how to best help set her clients up for future success, makes this book an absolute must read.

It is such a life hack to have a Mom who is in the business of money, someone whom I constantly learn from and bounce ideas off. To have this type of trusted source in my life is not something to be taken for granted, especially when you think about the amount of time and effort most people spend looking for a credible financial advisor. I am so excited for the world to have the type of access that I've been spoiled with for the last three decades. Do yourself a favor and tell a friend or two about this book.

I'm so proud of you, Mom. You're such an inspiration. Seeing you put in the work for this book, and hearing you speak of your work, it's so amazing. I am truly blessed to call you my Mother!!!!

Cliffton Sr., Coach Popovich, and Lynda

Coach Popovich and Brandon

BACKDROP

Pro Athletes' Career Perks and
the Sportin' Life Ecosystem

Pro athletes are enjoying increasing salaries, robust endorsement opportunities, and, because of the new lucrative collective bargaining agreements with some sports leagues, an increasing share of tournaments, and leagues' record revenues. According to a report by Ernst & Young published in 2022 and summarized on statista.com, the estimated annual revenue across the entire sports industry is expected to rise to $83.1 billion by 2023.[8] This projected growth is due to increasing fan interest, media-rights fees, internet broadcasting deals, expansion of smart monetization strategies in ticketing, innovative marketing schemes, merchandising and partnerships, e-sports, gaming, and daily fantasy leagues. This increasing revenue will undoubtedly allow elite athletes the opportunity to enjoy even higher salaries in the future. But will this economic windfall lead to a more secure financial future for all players?

Macrocosm Perceptions

We can all agree that pro athletes possess massive appeal. People want to hang out with them because they are fun to be around, are witty, have life experiences others do not, tell great stories, are usually very charming and charismatic, display lots of confidence, enjoy unadulterated entertainment, and like to party to mitigate stress, to entertain friends, and for partying's sake. Athletes have great physical presence and impressive athletic skills; they personify diligence, courage, and grit; they live aspirational lifestyles, have an expansive dating pool, and attract beautiful people at social gatherings; and they are usually very generous when it comes to gift giving and footing the hefty bar tab at clubs. In addition to an abundance of Twitter, Instagram, TikTok, and Snapchat followers, elite athletes have an impressive and oozing rolodex of friends and business associates like entertainers, politicians, and members of royal families. They get "free" stuff and are comped everywhere they go. They are mostly tolerated and gain widespread public acceptance to be outspoken and politically incorrect, can afford the best attorneys, and carry an international get-out-of-jail "free" card in their Gucci wallets. Their kabuki game is on another level.

On the flip side, professional athletes are envied by some and hated by "haters." Schadenfreude (pronounced *scha-den-freu-de*)—pleasure derived by someone from another person's misfortune—is a real thing. Sad truth: Some people can't help but feel pleasure when someone they envy gets their comeuppance. Studies have shown that episodes of schadenfreude light up areas of the brain where our reward system resides and play a major role in the release of dopamine, the "feel-good" chemical. This signifies haters' hate, because it feels good when something bad happens to someone they secretly envy or hate. When elite athletes fall on hard times, instead of eliciting empathy, some celebrate.

Show Me the Money

Professional athletes make good money; some people think they make too much money. One of the most colorful quotes in all of sports comes from retired Tampa Bay Buccaneers linebacker Warren Sapp, who once said, "We play a kid's game and get a king's ransom."[9] This quote has become a favorite of those in the media who wish to demonize young professional athletes for their high salaries. This quote may accurately depict Warren Sapp's feelings on his career earnings, but it does not necessarily depict the earnings reality of all professional athletes.

In 2017, Stephen Curry, a seven-time NBA All-Star who has been named the NBA League MVP twice and has helped his team win four NBA championships (2015, 2017, 2018, and 2022), signed a contract with the Golden State Warriors for a whopping $201 million over five years.[10] That's about $40 million a year, gross. But of course, this amount is an outlier, and many pro athletes do not make nearly as much. Despite some eye-catching, multimillion-dollar contracts, minimum rookie/veteran contracts for pro athletes are far less, as the following table shows.

Estimated Average Salaries for 2019–2020: Not COVID-19 Adjusted

NBA Average Annual Salary $8.32 Million –
Average duration in the sport? 4.5 years

MLB Average Annual Salary $4.03 Million –
Average duration in the sport? 5.6 years

NFL Average Annual Salary $3.26 Million –
Average duration in the sport? 3.3 years

NHL Average Annual Salary $3.07 Million –
Average duration in the sport? 4.7 years

Source: Average sports salaries by league 2019/20 | Statista[11]

To the average person hearing news about certain pro athletes' contracts, it may seem like they earn astronomical amounts. But many people tend to forget that published professional athletes' contract salaries and signing bonuses are *gross* amounts. After federal, state, county, and city taxes, the dreaded "jock tax," pension deferrals, agent fees, union dues, league escrow fees, and other fees and expenses unique to the sports profession, professional athletes actually do not make as much as you think. Athletes' actual take-home pay can be a mere fraction of the published contract figures.

> *"If you add up all the federal (taxes) and you look at the disability and the unemployment and the Social Security and the state (taxes), my tax rate's 62, 63 percent. So, I've got to make some decisions on what I'm going to do."*[12]
>
> —Phil Mickelson, pro golfer and three-time Masters Tournament winner

Adding to the tax woes impassionedly expressed by Phil Mickelson, there are other expenses athletes have to fork out to maintain or enhance their lifestyles and professional brands. Trainers, personal chefs, personal assistants, private transportation, security personnel, and remote living quarters - all come with high price tags.

Capitalism is alive and well in America, as professional sports is a massively successful business model and is enormously profitable with a wide fan appeal. Franchise owners, tournament organizers, and league leadership make a boatload of money—some hundreds of millions, and some billions, of dollars. All totaled, these fortunes are amassed from the talents of their at-will employees: the elite athletes. For the privilege of watching competition performed at the highest level, fans willingly pay high prices for tickets, parking ransoms at stadiums, $13 beers, $22 hot dog and fries combos, hats, hoodies, player jerseys, and other team-branded apparel, paraphernalia, and souvenirs that are sold everywhere. Vendors lease space at publicly subsidized stadiums to sell cool gear, multibillion-dollar deals are made with cable, internet, and TV networks to broadcast games, and there are video game licensing deals, and other team- and sport-related revenue streams limited only by the imagination of the sports' executives.

With all this cash flowing, many are in agreement team owners and tournament organizers can afford to pay large contracts to the athletes who train relentlessly to compete at the highest level, delivering exceptional live entertainment to the world. Is it better that the billionaire owners and sports league executives keep the bulk of the revenue for themselves and for their families? Or should they generously share the revenues with the hardworking athletes who trained most of their lives to make these revenues possible? Players' salaries reflect the value they provide and should be a fair share of this massively successful business of professional sports. Without the players, the sportin' community simply would not exist.

> *"The biggest thrill wasn't in winning on Sunday but in meeting the payroll on Monday."* [13]
>
> —Art Rooney, founder and owner of the Pittsburgh Steelers (NFL)

INTRODUCTION

The Jumpoff

The pandemic disrupted every aspect of our human existence, especially our financial lives. With the worldwide economic shutdown, many segments of the population were in for a rough year financially, even well-resourced professional athletes. The ramification of canceling or postponing live sporting competitions meant many athletes would need to find a way to manage without a regular paycheck or cash that would normally come in from product endorsements and appearances. During the summer of 2020, when the NBA restarted its 2019–2020 season (which went on hiatus in March 2020 due to the COVID-19 pandemic), rumors started to spread about certain NBA players being barely able to make it to the next payday.

Debates erupted on social media platforms about how it could be feasible for some NBA players to be living paycheck to paycheck. We read in newspapers and hear on podcasts that another pro athlete is going broke and files for bankruptcy after earning millions in his sports career. What is going on? "If you take the top 10% of all wage earners in professional sports out, about 90% are in financial distress, five years after they retire,"[14] according to author and financial advisor Ed Butowsky. *What?* There is not a lot of hard data out there on the personal finance misfortunes of pro athletes—only public bankruptcy records and public and private comments made by financial gatekeepers and pro athletes themselves. Hidden in plain sight behind the empirical evidence lurks a very troubling narrative.

Despite robust average annual salaries, according to a *Sports Illustrated* article published a few years ago, an estimated 60% of NBA players, 78% of NFL players, and a large percentage of MLB players go bankrupt within five years after leaving their sport.[15] The factors contributing to this perplexing money-management phenomenon are numerous. Similarly, many articles report an estimated one-third of lottery winners go bankrupt within a few years of their big winnings, and other celebrities and entertainers, even A-listers who have had incredible success and lucrative careers, run into financial difficulties leading to bankruptcies. Riches-to-rags stories of the rich and famous have been chronicled over the years in books, songs, movies, and TV comedies. So many people talk *about* the financial missteps of professional athletes in traditional media, on social media, in digital chat rooms, and in barbershops around the world. Their financial woes have even been comedic fodder for late-night talk shows. But who is talking *to* professional athletes about how to do a tribal course-correct? It's time to press the reset button. I'm calling a *mulligan!*

The real problem, as I see it, is financial literacy, or the lack of it. The solutions to address financial illiteracy may be straightforward, but the implementation and execution of an appropriate game plan to tackle this wealth-stealing pariah is not easy. Since the *Sports Illustrated* article was published, professional sports players' associations have created financial literacy/wellness programs for their members, but are they effective? Many financial literacy programs fail because they mostly focus on the numbers and learning formulas. Very few programs focus on changing behaviors. This book will change all of that. I put professional athletes' behaviors under the microscope to identify issues with the way money is thought about and make suggestions about how to make sound money moves to achieve better financial outcomes.

Money and psychology are often interrelated. It's been highly publicized that when some elite pro athletes get their first big paycheck, they begin their journey of adjustment. They buy big houses for themselves and family members, luxury cars, designer clothes, and expensive jewelry—spending money fast and loose without thinking about setting aside a portion of their earnings for career contingencies or saving for their future selves. Trendy investment opportunities, such as investing in unvetted digital assets like Cryptocurrencies, Bitcoin or NFTs, or buying into an ownership interest in a restaurant or car dealership, can be very enticing business ventures for anyone, but especially for the young, impressionable newly crowned millionaire. In this age of instant messaging and ravenous appetite for status, instant gratification is inevitable. Why do some pro athletes find themselves in financial distress after making an insane amount of money over the span of their sport careers?

It's Complex

Human behavior is complex, with many dimensions. Pro athletes have circumstances that are unique to their profession and make financial planning much different than other highly compensated professionals, such as:

- ➢ **Career span/frontloaded income.** Pro athletes have shorter earning time spans than those in other professions. During this time, their focus is primarily on performing well in their sport, not necessarily on sound money-management practices. They don't think about the need to have the money last a lifetime. Depending on the sport, the average age when the elite athlete receives the bulk of his earnings is 27 years old; the average retirement age is 33.[16] Pro athletes spend 20% of their life cycle making money that must last 50+ years. This leaves the retired athlete with a tough job of managing what they earned in the small earning window to last for the rest of their life.

- ➢ **Dopamine and compulsive spending.** Dopamine, a brain neurotransmitter/chemical messenger, is often called the pleasure chemical. Its primary role is to reinforce and reward pleasurable experiences, which can deceive the immature and undisciplined athlete to want more and more, and ultimately turn him into a compulsive spender, degenerate gambler, and father to many children who were not planned.

- ➢ **Physiology of the brain/cognitive immaturity.** According to research and the consensus of neuroscientists, the prefrontal cortex (the part of the brain associated with reasoned decisions, higher cognitive functions, controlled impulses, problem-solving, planning, short-term and long-term memory, emotions, creativeness, high-level communication, etc.) doesn't fully develop in males until the age of about 27.[17]

- ➢ **Unpredictable income streams.** Due to injuries, fierce job competition, shorter-than-expected professional careers, and contractual issues outside of their control, pro athletes may experience radical swings in personal income.

- ➢ **Massive and hungry entourages/posses.** Many professional athletes financially support family members, high school/college friends, and many others due to loyalty. The village is real.

> **Pressure placed on young players by veteran players, encouraging them to spend lavishly.** "For rookies, it's like an unspoken initiation—you're trying to get in good with the veterans, so you go beyond your means," according to Rod Strickland,[18] 17-year NBA guard.

> **Physically exhaustive work and demanding work schedules.** Active pro athletes literally have no time and seemingly little interest in learning sound money-management practices.

> **Lack of financial know-how.** Most pro athletes delegate and entrust financial/business affairs to "advisors."

> **Intimidation.** Financial terms and concepts are intimidating. They sound *Greek* to the novice.

> *"Once you get into the financial stuff, and it sounds like Japanese. They're lost."* [19]
>
> —Torii Hunter, retired MLB outfielder

> **Misplaced trust/unscrupulous advisors/unvetted business deals.**

> **Family matters.** Entitled family members, irremissible child support, and punishing divorce settlements are all common issues among pro athletes. Divorce can be costly for anyone, but especially for the highly compensated pro athlete. Regrettably many do not get prenuptial agreements.

Phenoms go from high school to college, where many "facilitators" are making most of their lifestyle decisions, including but not limited to what to do with their scholarship checks/stipends, where to eat, and who and how to date. These facilitators tell elite college athletes where to go, what to wear, what time to be here and what time to arrive there, and even what time to go to bed—leaving little need for athletes to make decisions on their own and removing the sense of agency, or the feeling of control. When these elite athletes turn pro and the big paycheck arrives, many are too inexperienced and cognitively immature to manage the transition from "protected" youth to business brand owner—the branded product being themselves. It's a daunting task for sure, and it can be overwhelming. At age 23 or younger, with a boatload of money, the elite athlete has not had enough learning experiences to gain the wisdom needed to manage this newly acquired wealth.

> *"Good judgment depends mostly on experience and experience usually comes from bad judgment."*[20]
>
> —Anonymous

At a time when executive skills of memory, emotional maturity, flexible thinking, and self-control are still forming in their young brains and with few true financial mentors or role models in the areas of sound money management, professional athletes fall prey to unscrupulous advisors and are sometimes ambushed and bullied into making unwise business decisions. They risk failing to realize the American Dream of financial independence after working so hard due in part to poor or misguided judgment and selfish or fraudulent acts of others—in other words, being taken advantage of. Pro athletes work hard during their short careers, adding value to their profession and to the teams that employ them; it's unfortunate that so many people in positions of influence take advantage of their youth and naivete. We all know there is a lack of focus on financial literacy in the U.S. formal education system. Added to this, the impatience and blind trust that youth brings, unbridled pride, and a healthy dose of ego and entitlement, the trap has been set and the unschooled pro athlete oftentimes finds himself ensnared in an unfamiliar web of duplicity—leading to financial disaster.

Financial IQ

According to a StrengthPlanet.com Fitness and Exercise Resource article and personalityanalysistest.com report, world-class athletes possess average to above-average IQs.[21] How, then, do seemingly intelligent athletes possess such a low level of financial literacy? How do they constantly fall prey to financial predators and succumb to financial miscues to end up broke? Pro athletes have access to the best of everything: the best trainers, the best mind coaches, and the best "advisors." Yet there are a myriad of well-documented stories of seasoned professional athletes who made poor financial decisions or were defrauded and suffered lifestyle-altering consequences.

> *"When you come into the NFL you are 21–22 years old, it's unrealistic to think that these guys, and I'm including myself, I was financially illiterate.*
>
> *You haven't experienced or worked long enough to know the differences between the right people to hire and evaluating an advisor or agent."*[22]
>
> —Zack Miller, NFL tight end

The past financial failures of fellow athletes *should* provide vicarious learning opportunities for newly crowned millionaires. One would believe this knowledge *should be* sufficiently effective to discourage poor financial decisions. However, this form of social learning requires that (1) these elite athletes are paying attention to the negative consequences of poor decisions made by others and (2) they internalize the consequences. This may be the problem: Pro athletes are so focused on their careers and being the best athletes, they simply have less capacity to be fully engaged in other parts of their personal and financial lives—plus their egos may marshal false confidence that these missteps won't happen to them.

According to the National Assessment of Adult Literacy, literacy has two components. One part of literacy focuses solely on knowledge.[23] This component involves word-level reading skills, such as recognizing words, or terms and concepts. In the case of financial literacy, this would include the ability to recognize numbers, math, financial terms, and formulas. The other part of literacy is the conceptual piece, which focuses on everyday tasks—the ability to use printed and written information to function in society, and to use this knowledge to manage financial resources effectively for a lifetime of financial well-being.

The first part of literacy is about mechanics (knowledge). The second part is about practical application (wisdom).

> *"Modern financial literacy efforts spend nearly all of their time on the knowledge piece. I've reviewed maybe a dozen FinLit programs over the years. Most pay no more than lip service to behavior, to the conceptual piece of financial literacy."*[24]
>
> —J.D. Roth, *Forbes* personal finance contributor and author

The math and mechanics of personal finance may not be that difficult. But understanding the psychological and behavioral side of money? That's hard.

Behavioral Finance/Economics

To make better decisions regarding money management, one needs a better level of knowledge both at the conscious and subconscious levels. Ninety-five percent of our behavior is influenced by our unconscious mind, which means only 5% of our thoughts and behaviors are controlled by our conscious mind. This is the exciting part of behavioral finance: the study, application, and influence of psychology on personal finances. The concepts discussed in this book focus on financial decisions made by young, newly crowned millionaires. Why do pro athletes go broke? When do we possess the cognitive maturity to make the best financial decisions? Why we do what we do with our money? To answer questions like these is the primary reason the field of behavior finance was developed in the 1980s. Behavioral finance explains human economic behavior, reveals our financial blind spots, and offers psychological tools we can use to make better financial decisions.

Money Beliefs

Our relationship with money is learned from our childhood, which is when we develop "money scripts®,"[25] a term coined by Brad Klontz, PhD, author, professor, and financial advisor. These "scripts" are our beliefs about money, which drive our financial behaviors. We might not be aware of many of these beliefs, as they are ingrained deep in our subconscious brain, and we are not conscious of their impact on decisions we make. "Money scripts® are shaped by our experiences with financial issues and parental attitudes, and ultimately shape our financial health,"[26] according to Dr. Klontz, from his research at Kansas State University.

Most of our mental processing and decision-making is unconscious, but that doesn't mean it's faulty, irrational, or bad. Our brains are faced with an overwhelming amount of data; 11 million pieces of data come into the brain every second,[27] according to social psychologist and author Timothy Wilson in his book *Strangers to Ourselves: Discovering the Adaptive Unconscious*. Our conscious minds cannot process all this data and, therefore, must rely on cognitive maturity and mental shortcuts or biases hardwired into our subconscious. Cognitive maturity makes us aware of multiple potential perspectives on any given situation, issue, or problem. The more mature we are, the more likely we will consider many factors when making decisions.

If it is true that most decisions are made unconsciously, what dictates how information gets processed and passed on from the unconscious mind into the conscious mind—to drive our behavior? And how can we manage this process so we can become better decision-makers? Understanding your own programming about money will be the lens through which you view the cognitive lessons outlined in this book. We all have been groomed to think about money in a certain way based on various factors. Among them are:

➤ Our upbringing,
➤ Modeling,
➤ Our social-economic background,
➤ The neighborhood we grew up in,
➤ Money topics discussed or not discussed in our homes,
➤ The friends we spent most of our time with,

> ➤ Our friends' families,
> ➤ Watching the "cool" kids at school,
> ➤ What we were allowed to read and what we did not read,
> ➤ The TV programs we watched as kids and young adults,
> ➤ If and how our parents talked to us about money,
> ➤ Watching our parents deal with money issues,
> ➤ If you received a true allowance or not, and even
> ➤ Whether you shopped for groceries with a parent or grandparent.

So many things influence our current money programming. This is also true for professional athletes. Decisions regarding money issues are influenced by our psychological programming and our "money script®."

Why I Wrote This Book

Failure is a gift. Penned in the format of corrective feedback, I wrote this book to help you, the elite athlete, do some introspection to discern your thinking about money, compare your own behavior to the mistakes of others, and help you learn from failure—either your own or the failures of others—to ultimately improve your financial outcome. Corrective feedback is how people learn from others in a group or tribe—about how behaviors, actions, style, strategies, and so forth are perceived by and affect others in the group. Many current pro athletes realize there is a stereotype of athletes being free spenders and oblivious to how their actions today impact their future. I am sure you are cognizant of the mistakes made by former players who played the excessive spending game and went broke; you don't want to make the same mistakes. Now it's your turn. You get to decide how the spending game should be played, and the world will be watching.

Can you learn from past behaviors of former pro athletes? Of course you can. You learn how to take care of your body to extend your professional sport careers from former players, how to choose the right sports agent, how to conduct yourself while on the field and in public, how to limit your time and engagement on social media, how *not* to choose a life mate, and more. Learning is transformative. No assertion is made that all pro athletes sprint to the cliff as far as handling their personal finances, nor are they guilty of making all 43 mistakes discussed in this book. But a significant number of elite athletes have made massive missteps with their personal finances. Some might even say epic blunders.

An effort was made to examine behavioral finance and cognitive maturity to answer two fundamental questions:

1. *Why* do we do what we do with our money?
2. How can we make better financial decisions?

In doing research for this book, I came across the term *G.I. Joe fallacy*,[28] coined by Laurie Santos and Tamar Gendler. The G.I. Joe fallacy refers to the misguided notion that knowing about a personal bias or error in judgment is enough to overcome it. In reality, knowing is *not* half the battle; information alone doesn't always change behavior. I believe sound money management is about knowing *and* doing. Being successful with money is as much about having actual knowledge about money as it is understanding your relationship and behavior with money. If you know better, you can do better, but the emphasis has to be placed on both: knowing and doing.

> *"It's good to learn from your mistakes. It's better to learn from other people's mistakes."*
>
> —Warren Buffett

Book Format

This book has eight chapters. Each chapter identifies different relationships you may have throughout your sports career and in life after sports: dealing with family and friends, professional advisors, self, and your entourage; managing mental and physical health; navigating the law; love; and life after your sports career. Within the eight chapters, I've outlined 43 ways *not* to handle your personal finances while providing ways to help you make better financial decisions, thereby improving your financial literacy. The best way to consume the contents of this book is to choose two or three points (reasons) that resonate with you, read each in its entirety, and then make a cognizant effort to make changes in your behavior on that topic as suggested. When time allows or a situation arises, continue to the next point (reason). Rinse and repeat. Increasing your financial literacy is not a sprint, it's a marathon—a delightful journey brimming with a-ha moments. After reading this book, your financial confidence will increase 10X and making poor financial decisions will be a thing of the past.

Why 43?

On January 10, 2012, my second son, Brandon, scored a collegiate career high 43 points to help the University of Illinois Fighting Illini upset No. 6 ranked Ohio State by a score of 79–74. Brandon went an impressive eight-for-10 from behind the arc and scored the team's last 15 points to close out the game. His full stat line: 43 points, 8 rebounds, 2 assists, 2 steals, and 4 gym-erupting blocked shots. My personal favorite stat: Brandon was 13 for 15 at the free-throw line—87%.[29] Yes! That game at the House of 'Paign, in Champaign, Illinois, was the most exciting basketball game I had ever watched in person. In honor of that victory and Brandon's impressive performance, I used 43 as the number of reasons. January 10, 2012, was a very special day for our family and for me, his former AAU coach. Ahhhh, the memories.

Finally . . .

While this book was written by examining the behavior of male pro athletes who were blessed with large sums of money, I hope all readers, regardless of your financial girth, can absorb a healthy dose of financial know-how and glean from the book's instructions on how to make better financial decisions, leading to better financial outcomes. Before we begin, I should mention: The purpose of my sharing this information is not to vilify the young pro athlete. To be clear, not all pro athletes make these mistakes, but a significant number of them are guilty of committing some of the financial *fouls* described in the body of this book. After doing the research for this writing, my first instinct is to hug the young athlete and assure him that making bad financial decisions is not all his fault. Next is to sit him down and have a firm, confidential conversation discussing a better way of doing things. Consider this informative read our sit-down session.

Whether you are blessed with a substantial stash, or just want to make better decisions to grow and protect the savings you have worked so hard to accumulate, these practical nuggets of wisdom can increase your financial literacy and help uplevel your financial decision-making. I am fully persuaded that this book will change your life. If I can encourage just one person *not* to make the same mistakes that are described in this book and to learn from the financial concepts discussed, then the 10 years I took to write this book will not have been in vain. It's time you made some sound money moves to help yourself to a better financial future. Ready. Set. Grow.

> *"Let the wise listen and add to their learning, and let the discerning get guidance."*
> —Proverbs 1:5 (NIV)

Learning is not enough; you must change your behavior to become financially literate.

> *"We learn wisdom from failure much more than from success. We often discover what will do, by finding out what will not do; and probably he who never made a mistake, never made a discovery."*[30]
> —Samuel Smiles, author and government reformer

CHAPTER 1

Dealing with Family and Friends

Having That Uncomfortable Conversation

Relationships are the currency of life. We value getting, being, and staying connected with people we love and care about. This connection provides emotional strength, trust, and respect. Relationships create a mutually beneficial system of support and helpfulness in the expansion of our human experience. Your family is an important part of your foundational beginning and emotional connectedness. Members of your family played critical roles in your life up until this point by helping to groom you to become the person and athlete you are today. As a young phenom in middle and high school, you started your ascent—a rising star armed with unique opportunities that propelled you onto the road to success.

Now you are enjoying a successful professional career, good money, and all the perks that come along with your profession and lifestyle. In contrast, many other athletically gifted youngsters unfortunately had a much different fate. Faced with obstacles, not opportunities, a less-than-ideal situation emerged that conspired to derail so many others, making it necessary to defer their dream of making it to big league, or to abort the dream altogether. Fortunately this is not how your story played out. With your family's help, you persevered. You are blessed and highly favored.

Family members, especially the support and influence of Mom and Dad, can make the difference in whether a young phenom stays the course to win the prize or implodes with regrets that could haunt a lifetime. Parents provide an environment for their young rising stars conducive to success. They make great sacrifices for the would-be pro to have all the opportunities to succeed, from taking them to practice, traveling around the country to compete in tournaments, scheduling specialized training sessions, making sure proper nutrition is available, shielding him from bad influences, helping him assemble a solid core of trusted advisors and trainers, and even seeking out personal mentors.

It's been well documented that having good friends in adolescence makes kids happier. One study from 2021 using data from more than 111,000 young people found that teenagers who were integrated into friendship networks had better mental health.[31] Extrapolating from that, student-athletes who cultivate relationships with team members, classmates, neighborhood homeboys, and besties are better equipped to handle the stress that comes along with attaining their goal of becoming a professional athlete.

Parents, siblings, friends, teammates, coaches, trainers, and mentors are all important members of the pro athlete's inner circle. Teamwork makes the dream work.

But what if the inner circle starts to crumble? When *kumbaya* is challenged and erodes into disharmony? What happens to these vital relationships when the pro athlete acts in ways that are detrimental to himself and his financial future? Well-meaning actions can jeopardize your financial future when dealing with family and friends—actions like becoming loyal to a fault to your peeps, surrounding yourself with yes men, transforming into a yes man, allowing yourself to be people-pleased, succumbing to lifestyle creep, crowning your talented barber as your agent and/or making him your power of attorney, and hiring family and friends as non-credentialed advisors. In this chapter we see how the inner circle can start to take on unpleasant characteristics that could lead to financial disaster.

> *The quality of human relationships is the greatest predictor of happiness, more than wealth, fame, success, or the number of love interests and it's also a huge predictor of health. Getting and keeping your financial house in order is a close second.[32]*
>
> —Lynda Paul, author and financial advisor

Family at the Spurs game

Family on vacation

Reason 1

Notoriously Loyal to a Fault

Remember when you learned that your dream of joining the professional ranks had finally come true? Maybe it was draft night. Maybe it was after a team-requested workout. Maybe you won a coveted amateur competition. Maybe it was during an open tryout with lots of talented athletes, and the GM called you aside to have a conversation. Or you got that long-awaited call from your agent: "Congratulations! You're in." Whenever and however it happened for you, like others before you, one of the first things you wanted to do is to share the good news with your family and a few of your closest friends. You defied the odds. You felt so proud that you did that thing—pure elation. With all that excitement, the discussion about the money soon followed. Yes! It's finally payday. You have now joined the elite community of the handsomely paid professional athletes.

Before you rush to social media to share how you spent your first $1 million, the best money move is to *pause* and take an assessment of your new reality. Less action, more thinking. No money moves should be made at this time, especially pre-commitments on how you plan to financially reward your inner circle for sticking with you throughout the grooming years. The worst thing you can do is to start buying things and making financial promises to others without having a clear financial game plan for how to handle the money, your family, and your friends. **There's power in the pause.**

"It takes a village" is an African proverb embracing the idea that an entire community of people must provide for and interact positively with children for those kids to grow in a safe and healthy environment. In the case of the professional athlete, the adage *it takes a village* is a good description of what it takes to help mature the elite athlete so he can attain the ranks as one of the best in the world. Kevin Garnett, who the Minnesota Timberwolves drafted straight out of high school in the 1995 NBA draft, is a great example of having a village of people to help him become successful. Garnett arrived at his new job at age 19 with a large contingent of family members and friends—affectionately called OBF (Official Block Family)—all of whom lived with Garnett in Minnesota. According to sports journalist and author L. Jon Wertheim, Garnett later credited his close friends and family for keeping him grounded and helping him thrive as a player.[33] A more recent example of the importance of family is a comment made by Klay Thompson, a four-time NBA champion with the Golden State Warriors, speaking of his brothers: "My brothers were definitely a huge influence because we would play so hard against each other in whatever sport it was. They allowed me to be the competitor I am today."[34]

During the most recent Olympics there were stories of families of Olympic athletes falling upon financial hard times while trying to provide an environment for their young Olympian that would be conducive for success. As mentioned earlier, family members make great sacrifices so the aspiring elite athlete can have the opportunity to succeed. Years later, after the lucrative professional contract is signed, it makes sense for the now-professional athlete to want to thank his immediate family and close friends for the love, support, encouragement, and belief they showed throughout the journey to achieve his dreams. In exchange for this enduring support, the pro athlete almost always wants to show his appreciation and repay his family's and besties' sacrifice by giving back financially to those who supported him.

There are two classes of advocates in what I affectionately call *The Entourage*: personal and professional.

Personal	Professional
Mom/Dad	Agent
Sisters/Brothers	Financial Advisor/Tax Advisor
Best friend/Homeboys	Banker/Business Manager/Attorney
The Posse	Trainer/Former Coaches

Personal assistant gatekeeper	Healthcare Team Sports Psychologist
High school/college friends	Publicist/Public Relations/Promoter
High school/college teammates	Chef/Nutritionist
Bodyguard/Problem-solver	Stylist/Barber

Pro athletes give their inner circle permission to shape them—knowingly or unknowingly. They help shape their thinking, behavior, convictions, and even their outlook on life. The one thing that is clear is this personal inner circle gives the pro athlete a sense of security. "Every professional player should have security. It's good to have some eyes in the back of your head,"[35] says LeBron James, speaking about the importance of his inner circle. According to countless articles on the internet, LeBron has the reputation as being very loyal to his inner circle. It's human nature to want to help or take care of someone you love, especially if they helped you reach a very important goal in life.

Understanding the sacrifices that were made by others on their behalf, pro athletes are grateful for the support of the many people who advocated for them throughout the process. Elite athletes are known to be very generous to many of these supporters—and spectacularly generous to the members of their inner circle. In some cases, this gratefulness-inspired benevolence can turn into deep loyalty to these individuals. Of course, loyalty is good; you should feel good about sharing and giving back in your own way. But if this benevolence gets out of control by not asserting boundaries and by allowing family and friends to take advantage of your kindness and generosity, you can find yourself in an uncomfortable situation of falling into a people-pleasing malaise.

Consider this: When you receive your first check, **pause**, assess your new reality, then create a carefully thought-out game plan that identifies how you plan to share your hard-earned money with your family and friends, those who supported you throughout your journey. Then communicate with members of your inner circle what you are comfortable doing and stick with that plan. You should guard against the need to give to family members and friends out of obligation or guilt. Base your generosity on what you can comfortably afford and what you can continue to do over a specified period of time. Don't allow yourself to be bullied into doing more. More is not always better. Before you communicate your gifting intentions, be sure to complete a thorough spending plan and consult with a trusted financial advisor to ensure you don't overextend your generosity.

Angel Capital: Investment Pool, Lending Pool, and Compassion Fund

Consider setting up and funding an investment pool, a lending pool, and a compassion fund, each with separate criteria. If a family member or close friend needs or desires funding, they would be required to present their case to a Family Advisory Board. The Family Advisory Board (FAB), made up of family members and friends, would decide as a team if that person should get the money for emergencies, perceived needs, or a business venture – something like the fam shark tank.

The investment pool and the lending pool should require a promissory note so family members understand there is an expectation to repay the pool—so there will be funds available for other family members for future needs and desires.

Once you fund the three pools with a one-time cash infusion, you should take a back seat and appoint a trusted family member to head the board and an independent third-party financial advisor to oversee the activities.

It is important that you are not involved with the day-to-day issues of the extended family's finances. You of course need to concentrate on your athletic career—and leave some nonessential family issues to others.

Once the pools have been exhausted, graciously decline additional financial support. This is a workable solution to deal with greedy or overindulging members of your inner circle.

Words to the wise:
Start the conversation about money with your family and close friends early.

Reason 2

Surrounded by Yes Men

You've reached this point on your professional journey by working hard and listening to advice from coaches, trainers, your inner circle, and others you trust. Many of these people, in their role as advocates, often agreed with you and the actions you were taking, only mildly offering dissenting opinions. Having people who support what you do and say is important; it helps you become confident in the general direction your life/professional career is taking. It's good to have agreeable friends and allies, but do you think it can be problematic to be so supported that your inner circle shies away from providing criticism when you deserve it? How beneficial do you think it is to have people around you put a pre-emptive stop to your potential bad decisions or bad behavior? Here's the rub as described by NFL Pro Bowler, and now college coach, Deion Sanders: "It's hard to talk to a person when they have millions, man, because there is so much noise in their life." Deion goes on to offer a possible solution, saying, "Everybody around them is employed and they have 'yes men.' You gotta start hiring a 'no man.' Somebody who is going to tell you no and somebody who is going to tell you the truth and a lot of these guys don't."[36]

Why does the profile-descriptive "yes man" bring up such a negative connotation? Yes man is frequently used in a derogatory manner to describe a person who is perceived to be overly agreeable and hesitant to share contrarian viewpoints, or someone who is amenable and docile. Vulgar slang views the yes man as a suck-up, brown-noser, or ass-kisser. According to the Farlex Dictionary of Idioms, a yes man is someone who always agrees with authority figures to gain favor with them; sometimes a derisive term suggesting that the person is a mindless follower of whomever they agree with.[37]

47

People in power have always surrounded themselves with yes men. For some, yes men are nice to have around because they appease the leader, they do not challenge decisions, they ask few questions, and they are generally compliant to authority. I get it. It's human nature to seek adulation and reinforcement rather than criticism. Legit, there are rewards for people who suck up to the boss. This agreeable disposition may place the yes man in a great position for a promotion or more of your face time, to maybe get invited to more parties, to earn additional social equity to cash in later. And since there's no secret that pro athletes often show loyalty for unwavering support by their yes entourage by providing financial support, some ass-kissers may be setting you up for a big payout later. This stealthy appeasement might translate into a new car, cash for business ventures, or even a new home. There are perks to kissing up, if the yes man is providing the required number of yeses.

This arrangement sounds like a win-win situation. At strategically appropriate times, the yes man interjects a tactical yes, here and there, giving the pro athlete accolades, reassurance, and affirmations. In exchange, the yes man earns a likeable reputation in hopes of garnering benefits from the pro athlete.

What's the harm? With all these yeses being thrown at you, over time you may start to feel sooooo good hearing the constant agreement—maybe to a point of becoming intoxicated. We humans want to be liked and likeable. The constant plaudits and affirmations serve as a nice surrogate for "They like me. They really, really like me." This repetition of yeses can lead you growing uncomfortable with dissent—leading to a posture: Agreement is good; disagreement is bad. Here is where the problem begins. By surrounding yourself with too many like-minded people, you will have little accountability for bad behavior and poor decision-making, including but certainly not limited to poor financial decisions, thereby hurting your professional brand. There will be no one to challenge you. Ultimately you will have no one to tell you the truth when the truth is needed.

On the flip side, some athletes not only surround themselves with yes men but they themselves become yes men. Case in point: As mentioned in Reason 1, pro athletes oftentimes demonstrate their loyalty by being very generous to their supporters.

Athletes say yes when asked to buy homes and cars for their mom, dad, and siblings.

- They say yes to family members and friends needing money for a seemingly endless list of wants and desires.
- They say yes to family members and friends wanting "loans" with no means to repay.
- They say yes to investing in "can't lose" business propositions.
- They say yes to investing in clothing lines, appealing to their unchecked, expanding ego.
- They say yes to investing in restaurant ventures without a vetted marketing plan.
- They say yes to investing in car dealerships.
- They say yes to giving gifts and loans to family and friends of love interests.
- They say yes to contributing to "get-rich-quick" schemes.

The drama begins when the claws of unsatiated appetite dig in and those who became accustomed to the yeses become entitled, expecting more and more. I hope this book is your peripety. Saying yes is a form of people pleasing. It should come as no surprise that many elite athletes are guilty of being people pleasers. They've lived their entire elite existence by pleasing people: coaches, trainers, parents, love interests, fans, and other supporters.

Test: If you become worried when you think one of your supporters might be mad at you or is disappointed in you because you didn't do something or give something they wanted, and in response you felt the need to do something right away to rectify the situation, your people-pleasing game is strong. This feeling that someone is mad at you can trigger a cascade of anxieties, causing you to feel overwhelmed and distracted. Disappointing people brings discomfort. Your initial reaction might be to try to find a way to course-correct or to fix the perceived kink in the relationship. Of course, these emotions are not good for the pro athlete who already has a lot on his mind. The eagerness to please can give rise to a fear of *"not enough-ness"* and, from a financial standpoint, this could lead to overcommitting financially, or making poor spending decisions resulting in unwise money moves and bad financial outcomes.

We all need some level of approvals and support from others. Studies have shown we are hardwired to seek acceptance and avoid rejection. Pro athletes are no exception. Because professional sports is a form of entertainment, pro athletes as the performers may require *more* approval from outsides sources than others. If you are always seeking approval from others, especially those in your inner circle, and are not supplied with a steady stream of desired reassurances, you might interpret this as they are disapproving of you, and you might start to feel disconnected from the very people you want to stay connected with. Assess your need to be liked and embrace the idea that you cannot please all people all the time.

Words to the wise:

Find a qualified "no" person—someone who will tell the truth. That might be a mentor, financial coach, trusted advisor, or friend. Understand that getting different points of view on financial matters can help you make sound money moves and mitigate potential bad outcomes.

Have at least one person (two is better) in your inner circle who will say, when it's appropriate:

"No, you should not go there."

"No, you shouldn't do that."

"No, don't buy that."

"No, that is a stupid idea."

"No, don't make that investment."

Hang around intellectual individuals who have the courage to tell you the truth.

Reason 3

People Pleased

You are making good money and you can buy just about anything you want. You are always surrounded by your old friends, a few new friends, and even a small group of hangers-on. A lot more people are trying to get your attention now. Everyone—especially strangers—is being so nice to you and going out of their way to do things for you. They give up their time and energy to get things for you, invite you to nice places, and introduce you to great people. It feels so nice to be "loved." Ever pause to ask yourself why? Maybe because they like doing nice things, or perhaps in hopes of earning your endearment, or maybe setting you up so you can owe them a favor later. Later = debt equity. Being the object of someone's affection may not sound all that bad. What's wrong with people being nice to you all the time and going out of their way to make you happy? Sharing one's time and energy to make someone happy may appear benign; you may even chalk it up to these individuals just enjoying your company. If you don't keep a watchful eye on these affection-seeking individuals, this admiration can take on controlling characteristics, as the people pleasers become more attached and overly possessive of your time and attention.

If you peel back the onion, people pleasing is a form of subtle manipulation. They want stuff. People pleasers often develop a sense of entitlement of expected benefits—quid pro quo. Don't get people pleased and fall prey to being manipulated, or you may become a victim of emotional and financial blackmail.

The life of a professional athlete is exciting. There are money and fame, you meet and socialize with exciting and attractive people, and you are invited to interesting events, introduced to provocative personalities, and privy to intriguing opportunities. The lifestyle can be intoxicating.

If you are not careful or grounded or do not have proper mentors, you can get consumed, lose touch with reality, and begin to think you are bigger than the lifestyle that surrounds you. You can get caught up, ensnared, and engulfed in the egotistical entrapment of wanting people to please you all the time.

With blinders on, you may be enticed to allow characters introduced to you by a friend of a friend to join your inner circle. Worse, you may even decide you need more superficial acquaintances than what is wise. New friends come with bags of intentions—and some with nefarious agendas. Use discernment before allowing new acquaintances, especially the seemingly innocuous people pleaser, into your inner circle. The combination of money and the need for "friendly" associates make professional athletes vulnerable to attract opportunists with criminal intent. Later in the book I talk about athletes being victims of fraud at a very high clip. Contrary to what you might think, the criminals who perpetrate crimes against athletes are often people who have befriended them, only to take advantage of the newly minted friendship later.

Words to the wise:
If you ever have an overwhelming feeling that people are being really nice to you, you may be falling into the trap of being "people pleased." This may be a set-up. Keep your inner circle small and be sure the people you trust lead transparent lives. Don't be naïve. Quid pro quo is a real thing.
Said in another way: Keep your inner circle small. The joint comes back faster.

Reason 4

Lifestyle Creep

You've worked hard and, now that you received your first paycheck, it's time to enjoy the fruits of your labor. People want to sell you things, and your friends want you to buy them things; pressure to spend money is all around you. Even teammates are putting pressure on you to spend money. Josh Childress, the sixth overall pick in the 2004 NBA draft, who signed a four-year rookie contract worth $11.7 million, shared that some of the veteran players he was around spent lavishly and encouraged him to do the same: "You get caught up in that and you end up spending more than you should."[38] The new lifestyle begins with a mindset—and maybe a little entitlement ("It's my turn")—and the tepid water starts to heat up, and so does the spending. It feels comfortable. *Lifestyle creep* is a term coined by Millennials to explain what happens when your income grows: Your discretionary spending increases, or creeps up, and luxury items become necessities. Things like upgraded living arrangements, premium gym memberships, and luxury cars all become non-optional. It's a new normal. Lifestyle creep can take the form of an ever-escalating taste for the finer things, putting upward pressure on regular monthly fixed expenditures. This insatiable appetite for mo' better diverts money from would-be savings. Beware. Here's where the comfortable water starts to boil, slowly.

Lifestyle creep happens to just about everyone. It happened to me back in the day. When I graduated from college in 1987, I was hired at Abbott Laboratories and agreed to a $27,000 annual salary (you can do the math to adjust for inflation). Added to my husband's income, this was serious money for us. We were officially DINKs (dual income, no kids). My husband and I looked for a townhome in the suburbs with the best school system, we upgraded our furniture and purchased new cars, then we went on our first real vacation to Disney World. We thought, "We earned the right to spurge a little"—and then the bills started to roll in.

Professional athletes certainly make more than $27,000 per year. They can easily earn in a single year or a few years what the average worker may not see in a lifetime. Making more money almost certainly means more spending. Athletes, being young and impressionable, and having received their first professional contract and subsequently their first real paycheck, can now experience "real" life for the first time; youth ushers in curiosity and exuberance. It's go time. I think I can speak for many professional money managers and financial advisors when I say we are advocates of the idea that pro athletes should give themselves permission to enjoy the lifestyle they have worked so hard to achieve. But you need to be careful not to overindulge.

Pro athletes make the same mistakes that others do when put in the position of a cash windfall, helping struggling friends and family members, and buying too many toys and aspirational designer clothes. But because they are extra, they start to treat themselves and their posse to gourmet meals at upscale restaurants, procuring salacious entertainment, purchasing more housing than they need, and acquiescing to compulsive gambling. It can become intoxicating. As the standard of living improves and increases, so does the spending.

In addition to the behavioral spending changes and increase in discretionary spending, there is a change in thinking. The athlete starts to believe that the spending on nonessentials items is a right rather than a choice. The mindset of entitlement is a real thing. The downside of lifestyle creep is when the income decreases, or when the professional athlete retires from his brief sports career and has to rein in his spending. It's inevitable. He may find it difficult to cut the spending and give up a portion of the consumptive lifestyle. This is a major reason why pro athletes go broke and become depressed. The best way to manage lifestyle creep is to create a budget—an income-appropriate monthly spending game plan—and live below your means during your professional career. Having an accountability partner and a financial advisor to help manage expenses and mitigate the mental indulgence jostling so the spending does not get out of hand is advisable.

> *"Spending money to show people how much money you have is the fastest way to have less money."* [39]
>
> —Morgan Housel, author,
> *The Psychology of Money*

Words to the wise:
Set spending boundaries. Spend way less than you earn.

Reason 5

Meet the Barber, the Power Broker

Should your barber act as your power of attorney? In legalese, a power of attorney (POA) is a document that authorizes another person to act on your behalf within the scopes defined in the document.[40] It is a very powerful document that, when certain conditions are met, gives your designated agent or attorney-in-fact access to financial information, to make business decisions, to open and close bank accounts, to legally bind you in business arrangements, even to authorize loans—simply put, to handle your financial and business affairs if you can't. In the wrong hands, however, this legal document can lead to financial devastation. Back in the day, some professional athletes regrettably signed over their power to their barbers, unscrupulous financial advisors, their agents, and even family members, allowing these characters to act in their stead using the rights granted in the power of attorney document. In many cases, this did not end well, indubitably leading to bad financial outcomes.

The power of attorney legal document, sometimes called a letter of attorney, is a written authorization to represent or act on another's behalf in private affairs, business, or some other legal matter. The person who gives or grants the power of attorney to another is authorizing the other to act as the principal or grantor or donor. For the purpose of this segment, it's the professional athlete. The person to whom the power is given is called the agent or attorney-in-fact.

Note: You do not have to be an attorney to be the agent/attorney-in-fact, anyone can be granted this power. *This is a big deal!* The agent is given the legal capacity to perform a task or tasks for the principal in his absence. A power of attorney can grant powers that may be very general, limited, or for a very specific business deal. When used properly, a power of attorney can protect your assets should you become incapacitated, and in some cases, it can free you from mundane matters in order to concentrate on more pressing matters. The power of attorney document is an essential part of any financial and estate plan, but before you sign over your rights, be sure the agent/attorney-in-fact is thoroughly vetted and has your best interest at heart.

There are four types of power of attorney:

1. **General:** This is a comprehensive, all-encompassing power of attorney. With this document, the professional athlete (the principal) essentially assigns all of his powers and rights to his agent. Proceed cautiously! Following are some activities that the designated agent can do when the general power of attorney is executed:
   ✓ Cash checks for the principal
   ✓ Manage all financial matters
   ✓ Manage all business matters
   ✓ File and answer lawsuits on behalf of the principal
   ✓ Make and enter into contracts on behalf of the principal

   The principal can revoke the General POA at any time, if he is of sound mind.

2. **Limited:** The power is assigned for a limited purpose: a specific date or an explicit transaction.

3. **Durable:** The major difference between the general and durable POA is the durable version is generally effective immediately upon signing and stays effective even if the principal becomes incapacitated. Because of these far-reaching and inexhaustible rights, the durable POA is considered the most powerful type of power of attorney.

4. **Springing:** This becomes effective only after a certain event or if the principal becomes incapacitated. Be aware that there are many legal definitions of *incapacitated*.

Note: With all types of POAs, the document becomes void at the death of the principal / grantor.

While skilled in hair design and skincare, I'm not sure your barber should have the legal prowess of a power of attorney agent/attorney-in-fact, unless qualified, properly vetted, and able to respect the degree of trust that has been bestowed upon him.

Words to the wise:
The POA in the wrong hands can place your personal assets at risk. Never sign a power of attorney unless you understand what legal powers you are abdicating, and you feel you absolutely need to. Proceed with caution.

Important subject matter disclaimer: A power of attorney (POA) is a legal juggernaut. The information provided in this section is not intended to constitute legal advice. Readers should contact their attorney or financial advisor to obtain advice with respect to any particular legal matter. No reader should act or refrain from acting based on information in this book without first seeking legal advice from their counsel in the relevant jurisdiction. Only your individual attorney can provide assurances that the information contained herein—and your interpretations of it—is applicable or appropriate to your situation.

Reason 6

Hiring Uncredentialed Family and Friends as Professional Advisors

What should you do when you are approached by a good friend or family member looking to become one of your trusted advisors? It is usually a bad idea to hire friends who lack the required skillset to do professional tasks. It is a better idea to keep friends for friends and, for business and financial matters, to hire skill and competence.

"It makes me sad I trusted someone I considered family to manage my money, and they did terribly wrong by me," said Dennis Rodman, NBA Hall of Famer, speaking on the financial fraud perpetrated by Peggy Fulford.[41]

Once an elite athlete gets on the pro potential radar, he starts to attract all kinds of people who call themselves "financial professionals." These so-called financial professionals vie for the athlete's allegiance and try to take on the role of either the sports agent or the financial advisor (or sometimes both). Family members and close family friends are notoriously guilty of trying to take on these advisory roles, as the family members/friends are the closest to the elite athlete and have already garnered his trust. The desire to please family and friends places the professional athlete in a precarious position: They love and trust family, but are family members qualified to do the job? Some former pro athletes hired people to fill these very important roles not because of their expertise, but because they're friends or family.

Help Wanted!

You will need a myriad of professional advisors if you are to thrive in professional sports. The three most important money management professionals are:

- A sports agent, to negotiate sport contracts and endorsement deals,
- A credentialed financial advisor, to help manage and invest your money, and
- A CPA or tax attorney, for tax planning and to file your federal and state tax returns.

These advisors *should not* be the same person. You don't have the professional expertise or time to oversee these very important activities, so it will be necessary to hire qualified professionals to fill these roles.

Sports Agent

Sports agents, in most sports, must have specific certifications just to be qualified to represent a professional athlete. The NFLPA (National Football League Players Association) requires individuals who wish to represent players and become a Certified Agent meet certain requirements before they can represent a player in the NFL.[42] The NFLPA requires would-be sports agents to have an undergraduate and post-graduate degree from an accredited college/university, successfully complete a proctored examination, attend a mandatory two-day seminar, agree to a background investigation, and pay a non-refundable application fee of $2,500.

The NBPA (National Basketball Players Association) requires agents who represent players to complete an application and pass a grueling Agent Certification Exam, agree to a background check, and pay a fee of $2,500.[43]

The MLBPA (Major League Baseball Players Association) requires agents who desire to represent players and become a Certified Agent to complete an application, agree for the MLBPA to conduct a background check, pass a written examination, and pay a $2,000 fee.[44]

Financial Planner / Financial Advisor

A CERTIFIED FINANCIAL PLANNER™ (a CFP®) is a certification[45] recognized in the United States and many other countries and is the standard of excellence in financial planning. The CFP® professional credential is known for its (1) high standard of professional education, (2) stringent code of conduct and standards of practice, and (3) ethical requirements that govern professional engagement with clients. All combined, these requirements reflect the commitment that all CFP® professionals make to high standards of competency and ethics. To attain the right to use the CFP® marks, an individual must satisfactorily fulfill the following requirements:

- ➤ **Education:** Attain a bachelor's degree and complete coursework on financial planning.
- ➤ **Examination:** Pass a comprehensive CFP® Certification Examination
- ➤ **Experience:** Complete at least 6,000 hours of professional experience related to the financial planning process, or 4,000 hours of apprenticeship experience that meets additional requirements.
- ➤ **Ethics:** Agree to be bound by the CFP Board's Code of Ethics and Standard of Professional Conduct.
- ➤ **Continuing Education (CE):** Complete 30 hours of continuing education hours each reporting period, including two hours of CFP Board approved Ethics CE.

CPA/Tax Attorney

To become a CPA[46] (Certified Public Accountant), an applicant is required to take the Uniform Certified Accountant (CPA) Examination to qualify for licensure as a Certified Public Accountant. The exam is a four-section, 16-hour assessment. CPAs are the only licensed accounting professionals. CPA licenses are issued by state boards of accountancy in the 55 U.S. jurisdictions. In addition to the Uniform Examination are an education requirement and experience. The CPA candidate must show completion of at least 150 college semester hours that includes 30 hours of accounting coursework and at least 20 hours each of core accounting subjects and related business courses. Public interest is protected when only qualified individuals are admitted into the profession. Tax attorneys generally have an undergraduate or master's degree in accounting and a JD.

Sports agency, financial advisory, and professional consultancy are serious business and should be left to qualified professionals with the proper certifications and experience. Recently constructed barriers to become a sports agent, and stringent requirements to be a CFP® and CPA/tax attorney, should deter many unqualified and uncredentialed friends and family members from applying for the coveted financial roles on your advisory management team. This is not to say that pro athletes should not consider a close friend or family member for one of these positions. Just be sure to properly vet anyone who applies for these very important positions to ensure they have the proper credentials, qualifications, and experience for the job.

Words to the wise:
Uncredentialed want-to-be advisors should go in the penalty box. Foul!

CHAPTER 2

Dealing with Professionals
and Your Money

Let's Get Down to Business

You've depended on others and expected them to do the right thing your entire life. Parents, friends, teachers, coaches, trainers, dining cafeteria waitstaff, crossing guards—all trusted "authorities" or "advisors." This deep-seated belief that people in authority will do what they say they will do, and in turn, you will be the benefactor of decisions made for your betterment is strong—is this naïve? This unbridled trust makes young elite athletes vulnerable to bad actors whose sole purpose is to prey on this naivete. Money reveals character flaws. Soon after an elite athlete signs his big contract, many with nefarious intentions show up to try to take advantage of this gullibility and blind trust. You spend most of your time preparing your mind, body, and psyche to put yourself in top condition to compete at the highest level. You are tenacious, committed, disciplined, focused, confident, and fully capable of taking your athletic gifts to the next level. This is your brand. Who has time to take care of the business side of professional sports and personal finances *to build* a professional brand, when you are so laser-focused on *creating* your personal brand?

You need a myriad of trainers and financial and business advisors to help maximize your athletic and financial potential. While you spend time training, competing, and curating your personal brand, advisors are needed to partner with you to do some heavy lifting to augment your professional brand. Who can you trust and, with a jam-packed schedule, how can you learn what you need to know to become a savvy brand curator for your sports career and your financial future? We read so often how pro athletes are defrauded by their "advisors" (not just financial advisors) and are either too embarrassed to pursue litigation or simply don't bother because they believe there are no funds left to recover. When the few muster up the courage to sue their deceitful advisors, they get more scorn than sympathy; the court of public opinion thinks pro athletes should know better. They are often given the disparaging title of "dumb jock" and barraged with social media commentary like "they should know better" and "when will they learn?" Learn what? That scumbags dressed in superficial cloaks of trusted "advisor" conspire relentlessly to take your money?

This chapter discusses the role of professional "advisors" and how to vet them before adding them to your inner circle. It's important to know how you can arm yourself with the knowledge to protect yourself, your mind, and your money so you do not become a victim of unscrupulous "advisors." Healthy skepticism should be embraced. Trust but verify.

Reason 7

Trust but Verify

"Stranger danger" is taught in schools across the nation under the D.A.R.E. program's marquee. Its premise is to warn students that all strangers can potentially be dangerous. In Malcolm Gladwell's book *Talking to Strangers*,[47] he points out that there is a difference in trust levels between younger people today versus people born in the Baby Boomer era. Baby Boomers have personally witnessed lies and the devastation that follow. Millennials (Yers) and Generation Zers are growing up in a world with seemingly less overt crime and have the internet to fact-check untruths if they desire. Gladwell's book dives into other reasons younger generations believe strangers, and he concludes his scientific and anecdotal walk-through historical evidence with this quote: "I think Millennials are very trusting. And when they say they're not . . . they're bullshitting." [48]

Millennial and younger generations are reverting to what author Tim Levine and other psychologists call "default to truth."[49] Young people assume that when someone says something, it's true—unless they *see* evidence to the contrary. They may be a bit naïve based on their age and lack of experience; they just don't have sufficient reason or knowledge or history to know when something is true or not true. This trust belief for elite athletes starts with the family and is extended to others, including coaches, school/team administrators, and people of authority. Trust is critical to sustain a positive relationship. This "default to truth" in relational circles make young elite athletes uniquely vulnerable to trusting the wrong people. Subject to cultural values and beliefs and conditioning, generally speaking, most young people are very willing to trust others without asking questions.

When entering or pursuing a new relationship, asking questions builds your emotional intelligence and allows you to make better character judgments. If you are not careful and you trust without asking pertinent questions, you can put yourself in a position to be exposed to exploitative treatment by those who are in positions of authority. To protect your personal and professional brand, do your own due diligence, safeguard your financial security, and do not delegate too much and oversee too little. Call your own shots.

> *"The simple believe anything, but the prudent give thought to their steps."*
> —Proverbs 14:15 (NIV)

Sidebar: A great way to assess the character of those who you do not know is to test them. Read *The Emperor's Seed* (author unknown) and create your own test. This idea was given to me by the Honorable Judge George Bridges in Waukegan, Illinois.

Words to the wise:
It's critically important to have a healthy dose of skepticism.

Reason 8

Million-Dollar Loans

Once you landed on the draft radar or started to hear your name buzzing around as a potential lottery pick, did anyone approach you to sign for a loan or cash advance prior to securing a professional contract? Yes? Then you know how professional athletes—who, according to their agent, assured by evidential matter from a GM that they will be drafted or signed—are aggressively and strategically approached by the enterprising lending community to promote opportunities for pre-contract cash advances. The amount of cash advances available can be as high as $250,000 (and in special cases even higher). Some elite athletes are given pre-draft lines of credit to cover training sessions, lodging, and incidentals in preparation for the draft. The terms of these pre-draft lines of credit are negotiated by the player's agent. If the communication channels are not transparent, an elite athlete could be surprised to learn that those funds were not gifts from his agent, but a loan that he will need to pay back (the cash advance with interest). Surprise! There are no free lunches in the big-boy sports business; everyone wants a piece of the action. Everyone.

Additionally, if the soon-to-be pro has substantial marketing clout, he can seek cash advances from companies to secure endorsement deals. In an interview with Graham Bensinger on YouTube, Shaquille O'Neal shared how he spent $1 million on cars for himself and his mother and father in one day after signing a $1 million endorsement deal—prior to the NBA draft and prior to hiring a financial advisor. He was later drafted as the #1 player in the 1992 NBA draft.[50]

Similarly, pro veterans who have been playing professionally for more than two years, and have guaranteed contracts, can get pre-approved cash advances as high as $2 million dollars or more based on the future value of the contract. Generally, these cash advances are used to give the player psychological momentum to train harder, to shore up his lifestyle, and/or to support family members who may be struggling due to the sacrifices they made to help the athlete attain professional status. Here's the rub: To receive this cash advance, the pro athlete signs a repayment agreement that may have high usurious terms or may have to pledge a high percentage of future guaranteed income. Ouch.

After a rookie signs a sports contact, some teams will give the athlete a signing advance—meaning they will give the athlete a portion of their salary up front upon signing their contract rather than having the athlete wait until the normal salary pay dates, which is spread out throughout the season. No interest is charged for advances given by the team, generally speaking. Pro athletes face many financial landmines due to their sudden wealth. Failure to create a workable spending plan (budget) and trusting the wrong people can become financially problematic. If you're not properly educated, these landmines can blow up and send a young, gifted star down the road to financial ruin. At the time of the printing of this book, many pro athletes who made millions of dollars over their playing careers, and are now retired, are still battling creditors in court over thousands and millions in unpaid loans and cash advances.

Be forewarned: Do not sign for cash advances and high-interest loans. Many reputable sports agents advise their pro athlete clients not to take these loan offers and tell them they are better off *waiting* until they sign their professional contracts to get a no-interest signing advance from their new team or endorsement deal. This is sound advice.

During the COVID-19 pandemic, many sport franchises and professional associations had to adjust business spending due to the economic shutdown. This meant league payrolls were cut substantially. There were a lot of rumors swirling around the sporting communities that many pro athletes had taken out loans at very high interest rates, using the funds just to survive, as well as stories of others living paycheck to paycheck. Professional athletes get accustomed to a certain lifestyle and some, well most feel obligated to help immediate and extended family members make ends meet. Those supposedly high-interest loans were probably their only option to do their best to stay afloat. This past economic shutdown was the best lesson on the importance of having a comprehensive financial plan that include a contingency plan, working budget/spending plan, and especially a provision for an emergency cash stash.

Following are types of advertisements used to lure pro athletes into cash advance loan arrangements or bridge funding debt instruments. These loans typically have arcane transaction fees, high interest rates, and onerous loan terms.

All Loans / Cash Advances
XXX Lender offers customized banking and financing solutions for professional athletes in the NFL, NBA, MLB, NHL, and MLS. We specialize in contract-based financing and contract advances and offer a wide range of financial products and athlete loans, including pre-draft loans and XX mortgages, designed exclusively for professional athletes. Repayment schedules are customized to match the athlete's complex needs.

Athlete Business Venture Financing
Many athletes use XX Loans to obtain loans used to finance business ventures to help secure their long-term earnings potentials.

Pre-Draft Financing
NFL and NBA draft-eligible prospects can receive financing prior to signing a professional contract. Eligibility is based upon a player's draft prediction and projected salary. Financing is available to athletes with no credit history, and funds can be available the next business day.

XX Mortgage for Athletes
Residential mortgages designed exclusively for professional athletes. Players can finance up to 110% of the purchase price of their home, which means players do not have any up-front out-of-pocket costs for a mortgage.

Free Agent and Arbitration Financing
Players exiting rookie or reentry-level contracts, or players approaching free agency are eligible for financing. Arbitration financing is available for MLB and NHL players while they await arbitration decisions and contracts.

Insurance Premium Financing
XX offers insurance premium financing and can help players obtain athlete insurance policies. Some of the disability insurance products available include loss of value, permanent total disability, and temporary total disability.
XX Lender works exclusively with athletes and entertainers to provide short-term early access to a portion of their future earnings using their guaranteed contracts or luxury assets as collateral.

Credit Cards

Carrying credit cards or some form of digital cash makes the purchasing experience very convenient. Credit cards for pro athletes have many benefits. They are portable, are accepted internationally, are fraud "protected" (generally you are not responsible for unauthorized purchases made by unauthorized users), have built-in rewards to encourage usage, and in some cases offer the ultimate spending freedom with no purchasing limits—yes, no limits (a la the American Express Centurion Black Card). On the flip side, there are costs associated with using credit cards, including transaction costs, fees, and interest. User beware—a word of caution about credit cards: At the top of credit card statements is a "minimum payment warning": *If you make only the minimum payment each period, you will pay more in interest, and it will take you longer to pay off your balance.* For example, if you have a credit card with an outstanding balance of $10,000, and the bank charges a 23% interest rate on the credit card, if only the minimum payment amount is paid every month, it will take 29 years and four months to pay off the total credit card balance. *Wow!* In this illustration, you would have paid more than $18,512.19 in interest and $10,000 in principal over that time, totaling $28,512.19. I hope the designer watch was worth it. Not all lenders use the same formula for calculating minimum payments, so if you are comparing offers, you can't expect to match the minimum amount due on one card with a different issuer. Most banks' minimum monthly payment formula is interest plus 1% of the balance. Following is an example of making only the minimum payment every month using the illustrated credit card balance of $10,000 and a 23% interest rate. The initial minimum monthly payment is $291.67. It will take 352 months (29 years and four months) to be rid of this debt, and over that time, you would have paid $18,512.19 in interest = total payoff of $28,512.19.

Payment Schedule (Abbreviated Monthly):

	Payment	Interest Paid	Principal Paid	Remaining Balance
Beginning Bal:				$10,000
Month 1	$292	$192	$100	$ 9,900
Month 12	$262	$172	$ 90	$ 8,864
Year 5 (End)	$161	$106	$ 55	$ 5,472
Year 10 (End)	$ 88	$ 58	$ 30	$ 2,994
Year 15 (End)	$ 49	$ 32	$ 17	$ 1,638
Year 20 (End)	$ 26	$ 17	$ 9	$ 896
Year 25 (End)	$ 15	$ 9	$ 6	$ 489
Year 29.4 (Last)	$ 10	$ 0	$ 10	$ 0

Note: Bankrate.com Credit Card Calculator was used to create this chart.

The detrimental effects of high credit card interest have been discussed ad nauseam by the financial community, but credit card holders still rack up the non-emergency charges on high-interest credit cards. Why do we make financial decisions that are not in our best interest?

Primarily, because we are not always rational beings—and in truth, we want what we want, and we want it as soon as possible. Studies suggest plastic numbs us, makes us complacent, and makes us likely to spend more.[51] Translation: Our brains experience a pain-like reaction to the immediacy of using cash, so we prefer using credit cards over cash.

Vendors know something you may not: When we use credit cards, we spend more—an average of 23% more. This is why you are getting so many credit card offers in the mail, offering credit cards and encouraging charging activities is very profitable to banks. We know that charging large sums of money on a high-interest credit cards, when it's not an emergency, is the worst decision ever—and yet we do it anyway. When we get the monthly statement, we regret having made that financial decision to charge. We just can't understand why we made such a bad decision. Miraculously, much to our chagrin, we do it again, and again, and again.

Student Loans

Some student-athletes leave college with student loan debt. Most full-ride athletic scholarships cover tuition, room and board (housing and food), and a stipend for books. But as many know, attending college requires more discretionary funds than these essentials. Depending on the amount of their athletic grant-in-aid provided by the university, some college athletes use funds from their student loans to cover the cost of their apartments, cell phone, video games, date nights with their girlfriend(s), car payments, car insurance, and that rare opportunity during breaks to travel home to visit family. This buildup of student loan debt is not a problem if they are the lucky ones to get a pro contract after leaving the university. But what if the student-athlete leaves his undergraduate college/university with no pro contract, no college degree, no job prospect, and a mountain of student loan debt?

By borrowing wisely and fully understanding his debt obligations and repayment requirements, the student-athlete can stay on track and empower himself to make the most of his time at school. But what if a student-athlete uses student loan debt for expenses that the loan was not intended to cover? The most egregious case of ill-advised student loan debt accumulation was someone who contacted me to discuss his financial situation. He had more than $350,000 in student loan debt. He graduated but went undrafted and wanted to pursue a master's degree in counseling while looking to earn an NFL contract as a free agent. By the numbers: With a $350,000 student loan, if paying the minimum amount monthly at 6% interest, this athlete will need to repay $3,885.72 every month, and it will take 10 years to pay off this debt in full. Ouch! Sorry, no Biden student loan forgiveness for you.

Are You in Debt Trouble Now?

If you find yourself in a hole, the first thing to do is stop digging. If you are in debt trouble, it is best to stop using your credit cards and get credit counseling right away. Abstain from overspending until you have addressed the actions that got you into this situation. I have always been intrigued by the idea of sanctioned silent torture or slow inevitable death that is escapable, particularly the kind personified by the urban parable of the boiling frog.

The Legend of the Boiling Frog

If you put a frog in a pot filled with pleasantly warm water and gradually heat it, the frog will remain in the water until it boils to death. There is a parallel to the fate of those who live life financially illiterate, oblivious to the consequences of poor financial decisions.

The adventure feels comfortable at first, then one day you find yourself broke—void of financial resources to climb out of the proverbial financial hot water.

Why allow this to happen? It's like financial death by a thousand burns. Stop your errant ways and make a commitment today to do what is necessary to give yourself the best chance at a financially secure future. Don't wait until the heat is turnt up. Jump!

Words to the wise:
If you are a credit-card-carrying member of the human race, and many of us are, try to live within or below your means and only use your card for the convenience feature.
Charge only up to the amount you can comfortably afford to pay off at the end of the month. If you have an unforeseen emergency and need to use your credit card to the maximum limit, forego some lifestyle luxuries until the debt is paid off in full. Building a rainy-day cash fund for emergencies is prudent and a sound money move.

Reason 9

Do-it-All Sports Agent

Your agent plays a very important role in your sport's career. Working as your career manager, your agent represents you during contract negotiations, handles all team-related business issues, and helps procure additional sources of income for you, including endorsement deals and special paid appearance opportunities. Your agent works around the clock to help maintain your public image and is the protector of your professional brand. At the appropriate time, your agent provides career guidance and prepares you for a career after retiring from the sport. With all these responsibilities, I can't image the sports agent also taking on the role as business manager, publicist, financial advisor, and tax advisor. Unfortunately, some do. You need to consider deploying a team of advisors and not depend on your agent to be a jack-of-all-trades.

The Management Advisory Team

With increasing salaries, business demands off the field, outside endorsement opportunities, and numerous activities "after the game," professional athletes are like small businesses. You already know that hiring a financial advisor/professional money manager is advisable, but many elite athletes may not realize that, to maximize their business potential, they need other qualified professionals to perform other needed services. While you're busy perfecting your athletic talents and jockeying for a leadership role on the squad or position rankings, your management team should coordinate efforts to handle ways to maximize financial revenue, legally limit tax exposure, aggressively manage your social media reputation, and help keep your personal life in order.

The business manager (personal assistant) handles many personal issues for the professional athlete: coordinate schedules, make dinner reservations, pay bills, manage home needs, facilitate family requests, pick up clothes from the dry cleaner, do personal shopping, get cars detailed, etc. This role is sometimes referred to as the *vice president of operations for the small business professional athlete.*

The publicist (brand purveyor) generates and manages favorable publicity and images for the professional athlete to enhance his image and is generally a public relations specialist. They handle media relations, solicit media attention, set up interviews, and other reputation-enhancing engagements.

The financial advisor (financial planner/financial advisor) is a qualified financial professional who helps individuals plan for their financial futures. Primarily they are Certified Financial Planner® professionals (as discussed in Reason #6) and either own their own financial planning practice as a Registered Investment Adviser (RIA) or work for a bank or a brokerage firm. Pro athletes need help navigating the unique challenges of instant wealth and help evaluating business and investment opportunities. The role of the financial advisor includes but is not limited to bringing together resources for innovative cash management, wealth protection, goal-based financial strategies, post-career planning, and retirement, estate, and multi-generational wealth planning. The financial advisor's main goal is to ensure they execute their client's plans for a rewarding current financial existence and a successful financial future. I affectionately call this the "now and later approach" to creating a lifelong financial plan. See Reason #10 and Reason #11 for more information on choosing a financial advisor.

The tax advisor offers professional athletes qualified advice to navigate the vast and complicated IRS tax code, executes tax strategies to legally reduce tax liabilities to retain as much of their earnings as possible, knows which state to have tax domicile as to maximize state tax savings, audits and reconciles the "jock tax," and prepares annual state and federal tax returns. The tax advisor should work with the business attorney to protect the athlete's business interests and the financial advisor to maximize tax-efficient investment opportunities.

The dedicated private banker provides special attention by offering concierge treatment with personalized banking products including high-yielding savings accounts, loans with favorable terms, and cash-management strategies, along with alias account names to protect your identity.

Attorneys on your team might include access to a tax attorney, business and contract law attorney, real estate attorney, family law attorney, intellectual property attorney, and, when appropriate, criminal defense attorney.

Words to the wise:
Delegate professional tasks based on verified expertise, not friendship.

Reason 10

The Vetting Game

There's chatter that some pro athletes spend more time researching gadgets to include in their perfect ride than they do finding a suitable financial advisor. If there's any truth to this, after you've built that awesome dream car on your fave customization website, you will need help negotiating an appropriate price to pay and whether you should use cash or obtain financing to acquire your new vehicle. More important than that new ride, you will need assistance navigating the unique challenges of instant wealth and evaluating business and investment opportunities. A qualified financial advisor will not only help you navigate the landscape of big-ticket items, but bring together resources for innovative cash management, goal-based financial strategies, and retirement, estate, and multigenerational wealth planning. A qualified financial advisor has the competence to help their client invest better and budget smarter, and to encourage him to spend *much* less than he makes.

The financial advisor's main goals are to help you establish your priorities and create a customized comprehensive plan for a financially successful future. A financial advisor is without a doubt one of the most important persons on your management team. The importance of vetting the financial advisor cannot be stressed enough. A comprehensive questionnaire should be completed, and thorough homework should be done before you hire your financial advisor.

According to the U.S. Bureau of Labor Statistics, as of September 8, 2022, 330,300 people in the labor market call themselves a financial advisor.[52] The term *financial advisor* isn't an official title or name or degree. It's a generic name for people who provide a wide variety of financial services. There is no formal degree required to be a financial advisor. Anyone can call themselves a financial advisor—and many do. Financial advisors don't have to have specific licensing requirements, but some licenses and certifications signal that the financial advisor is a true specialist and has professional oversight to hold them accountable. According to financial guru and radio personality Dave Ramsey, the following are well recognized credentials: Certified Public Accountant (CPA), Personal Finance Specialist (PFS), Registered Investment Adviser (RIA), Chartered Financial Analytics (CFA), and Certified Financial Planner™ (CFP®). High-quality credentials have prerequisites, substantial curriculums, proctored examinations, and continuing education requirements before someone is allowed to don the title. For example, the Certified Financial Planner™ CFP® credential demonstrates that an advisor has completed a rigorous process to become a financial advisor. See Reason #6 for more details on CFP® credentialing.

After identifying some financial needs, wants, and desires, consider the following checklist to vet a financial advisor to discern whether they are a charismatic salesperson or a substantively trained, experienced advisor:

- ✓ Check the advisor's credentials.
- ✓ Verify the advisor's educational background.
- ✓ Review the advisor's experience.
- ✓ Review whether there are any client/public complaints.
- ✓ Ask about the advisor's personal and professional philosophies.
- ✓ Search the advisor's regulatory history, proper industry licenses, and certification(s).
- ✓ Understand the advisor's given title (industry-specific or given by the company for status).
- ✓ Understand fees and how the advisor is compensated.
- ✓ Know the advisor's expertise.
- ✓ Conduct legal background checks on the advisor and their assistants (screening for recent bankruptcies).
- ✓ Know if there are any conflicts of interest (e.g., if they receive higher commissions for selling proprietary financial products, as compared to third-party financial products).
- ✓ Run potential advisors' names through FINRA's tool, BrokerCheck. This online tool is primarily for commissioned brokers. Independent RIAs may not be listed here.
- ✓ Check out the SEC Investment Advisor Public Disclosure website for Independent RIAs.
- ✓ Request the most current ADV firm brochure from the RIA firm you are looking to vet.

✓ Understand the difference between a fiduciary and non-fiduciary commissioned broker.

With its arcane qualities—so many different titles given to financial advisors, incessant fee-based service offerings, sales personnel pitching high-commissioned proprietary financial products, and bad advice/self-serving doubletalk—it may appear that the financial advisory community is rigged to set individuals up for failure. The industry is confusing at best—and at its worst may intentionally be stacked against the novice, not necessarily for him to fail, but to keep him sufficiently in the dark to make it necessary for the young, inexperienced investor to reach out for assistance. Bad advisors are not necessarily bad people. They may have great personalities and may be extremely cordial. Unfortunately, these character traits have nothing to do with competence or ethics. The most dangerous advisors may also be very likeable and possess exceptional sales skills. You need to discern if the advisors who want your business are well-groomed salespeople or trained, experienced financial advisors. Do the work. It's important for the fate of your finances.

Watch out for financial advisors with fake credentials. Do not be too impressed or deceived by a long string of letters after someone's name. Properly vet anyone who applies for the job to be your financial advisor by making sure they have the *proper* credentials, competence, qualifications, and experience. And yes, character matters. Be careful not to give your newly hired financial advisor too much control. Know the term *discretionary* as it relates to your investment portfolio, do not sign a power of attorney document until you are fully aware of what you are signing, and take an active role in managing your own finances. Call your own shots.

Words to the wise:
Always insist the financial advisor you hire has proper credentials and experience, not just a friendly smile and a dope suit. Request a letter of engagement.

Reason 11

Just Answer 3 Questions, Please

You might be asking yourself why you should pay a financial advisor when you could manage your money yourself. Managing money is a daunting task. There are so many landmines that can trip you up, like hidden fees, deferred charges, and other financial or tax ramifications – passively eager to confront the unknowing / uninformed. It's too important to take this task likely. The lingo alone can be very intimidating. Financial advisors play a very important role in helping you understand how to navigate the vast financial landscape. Their insights should be valued. Having the right financial advisor is not just about getting assistance with managing investments, not just about creating tax-efficient wealth-accumulation strategies, and not just helping you effectively engage with attorneys and other members of the business community or even selecting the right kinds/amounts of insurance to help transfer financial risks. Once you determine your priorities, a financial advisor can help you balance your cash-flow needs between current lifestyle preferences and building and implementing an integrated financial plan to achieve your long-term financial objectives. Sound money management includes things like goal-based saving strategies and tactical approaches to cash-flow management, especially between your sports career and life after sports.

Financial literacy shapes the demand for financial advice and improves the quality of the financial advice acquired.[53] It's not just about money. Professional financial counseling can give you a psychological boost that could make you more confident and happier by reducing stress and freeing up your time to focus on things that matter to you, ultimately leading to a peace of mind. Financial planning can lead to better decision-making, more money saved, less financial risk, and better financial outcomes. A financial advisor keeps you on track to meeting your financial goals throughout life's many cyclical turns.

After vetting the financial advisor's credentials and background, here are the three most important questions to ask before hiring a financial advisor/financial planner:

1. How are you paid?
2. Are you a fiduciary?
3. Are there any conflicts of interest?

"How Are You Paid?"

You wouldn't hire a yard maintenance professional without knowing the cost of their service, yet more than one in five investors—21%—don't know what they pay in investment and advisory fees, according to a survey by Personal Capital.[54] Based on my personal experience as a financial planner, I believe this 21% is grossly understated; the percentage is probably much higher. It's important to know that financial professionals are paid in a myriad of ways:

- Commissions—based on products sold
- Fees—based on time/advice/professional expertise
- Investment product fees like 12b-1 fees/trading fees
- Financial plan flat fee/oversight management fee
- Percentage of assets under management (AUM)
- Bifurcated fee schedule/embedded transaction fees
- Fee-only or fee-based
- Planning fee plus commissions

When vetting a financial advisor, you should ask: *What are my total all-in costs if I engage to work with you—including the fees charged by the investment asset managers?* Generally, to compensate themselves for their time to manage money, the average financial advisor charges an annual fee of 1% of assets under management (AUM). The firm that the advisor works for also charges a fee based on assets under management, and the custodian of the funds another fee. Every investor should know how much their financial advisor costs and how much the investments cost. Otherwise, how can you evaluate whether the services and the products are worth the money?

"Are You a Fiduciary?" [55]

Generally, a fiduciary in the financial arena is an organization that or someone who acts on behalf of another person, putting their client's interests ahead of their own, with a duty to preserve good faith and trust. Fiduciaries are bound both legally and ethically to act in the client's best interest, without exception. Registered Investment Advisers (RIAs) are advisory firms that have a fiduciary duty to clients; commissioned brokers at broker-dealers only have to meet a less-stringent suitability standard, which does not require the advisor employed by the broker-dealer to put the client's interests ahead of their own. Suffice to say, only hire a professional money manager who is a fiduciary. A fiduciary:

- Acts only in the client's best interest.
- Manages the client's money and property carefully.
- Keeps the client's money and property separate from her own.
- Keeps good and transparent record of accounts.

"Are There Any Conflicts of Interest?"

Conflicts abound. We live in a world with complicated business / financial systems. It seems everything has some interconnection; therefore, some conflicts cannot be avoided—but they should be disclosed and managed to the benefit of the paying client. A conflict occurs when the financial advisor and the professional athlete have competing interests. These different interests have the potential to financially harm the pro athlete's personal finances and/or business dealings. Some conflicts are housed as excessive risks, the firm's compensation arrangements, how the advisor gets paid, substantial personal gain from a referral, proprietary products that pay the advisor a higher commission compared to a non-proprietary competitive product, or other self-dealings with an affiliated third party. A conflict of interest may be an actual conflict or a potential conflict, and it can arise before the business proposition is accepted or at any time during the engagement.

A competent professional advisor should have business systems in place for managing conflicts of interest if they should arise. In business engagements, it's human nature to not share potentially damaging information when selling products and services, out of fear of losing the deal. A lack of transparency should be expected in some business deals. However, if you—the pro athlete—ask this question about conflicts and get the answer in writing, you will give yourself some legal protection if you lose large sums of money from the transaction due to lack of disclosure. If the financial advisor has a material conflict of interest with you that could affect your professional relationship and/or your financial interests, there should be an obligation to disclose the conflict and find ways to mitigate the conflict to your benefit. In all business engagements, you should always ask the question about conflicts of interest and get the response in writing.

Words to the wise:
Some people are offended when you ask questions about a service they provide. Before you retreat at their offense, you need to remember that it's your money, it's your decision, and it's your prerogative to ask questions. Asking questions doesn't necessarily mean you don't know the answers; asking questions gives you the confidence that others know what they are talking about. Question everything.

Reason 12

Background Checks

With increasing salaries, outside endorsement opportunities, and the status of social media influencers, professional athletes are like small businesses. Bringing a partner into the business can bolster the skills and synergistic technical expertise of the team and can be one of the best strategic and financially sound moves to increase revenue opportunities. A comprehensive business partner background check is the best way to protect you from fraud and deception, and to ensure all is being done to prevent unforeseen negative issues from cropping up in the relationship and future business dealings. It's common for business partner candidates to present themselves in the best possible light. This could mean potential business partners neglect to mention adverse information or something that you should or need to know. It's in your best interest to perform all the due diligence up front, before the business union is formalized.

A background check can reveal negative financial circumstances, poor credit, past bankruptcies, or a pending lawsuit that could cause the would-be partner to be a liability instead of an asset. Important questions that can be answered with a thorough background check include: if the candidate is lying about their credentials or if their presentation has misrepresentations, if the would-be partner was involved in a criminal proceeding with negative ramifications, or if there is a substantial difference in value systems. Additionally, a result of an investigative deep dive may reveal negative revelations about former business dealings. A potential partner's personal IRS or state tax issues could potentially have an unexpected consequence on the new partnership arrangement. If the partner candidate has unresolved financial issues, they might siphon unauthorized funds from the newly brokered partnership if they find themselves in a financial jam.

These are just a few of the issues you should be aware of before forging ahead with a business partnership. Once the background check is done and the results are reviewed, contractually, the written report could expedite any legal recourse to dissolve the partnership if your new partner's behavior does not live up to ethical or professional standards. CYA.

Considering Entrepreneurship?

No partnership, no problem. Time permitting, you can opt to go it alone and seek your own business deals without taking on partners and without sharing the potential profits or paying agency fees. If you go this route, decide if you have the time needed to pursue the business deal, then determine if you have the intellectual capital, professional leverage, and negotiation skills to get the deals done. *What's the best way to protect your assets in business dealings?* As a prudent precautionary measure, you should consider creating a legal corporate entity for all business transactions (i.e., a professional corporation, PSC, C-corp, LLC, or S-corp). Incorporating protects personal assets by separating them from those of the business. In the event of a lawsuit or a company bankruptcy, your personal assets would not be at risk. Additionally, a letter of indemnity should be used in business transactions to assure you will not suffer a financial loss if the other party cannot fulfill parts of an agreement. Business attorneys and CPAs are best suited to guide you as to which corporate identity you should pursue.

Words to the wise:
That unsavory associate is counting on you not doing a background check.

"The man who complains about the way the ball bounces is likely to be the one who dropped it."[56]
—Lou Holtz, former Notre Dame football coach

Reason 13

Second Opinions

Whether you are presented with a proposal for a potentially lucrative business opportunity or need to select a personal investment manager, analyzing such engagements is critically important, as the devil is always in the details. Some business proposals include *potential* growth projections and unproven strategies. If you're evaluating investment professionals, know that most investment advisory proposals include *sample* portfolios, *estimated* annual costs, and *historical* performance—all guesstimates; past performance is not an indicator of future results. Sometimes it can be very difficult to know if the presented proposal is the right fit for your needs. The best way to thoroughly review a project/professional advisory proposal is to compare it with a similar project/proposal by way of a second opinion from an unaffiliated third party.

What if the initial advice you receive in a business dealing is bad advice? If there is only one source to evaluate the advice, then you may never know if the information is faulty or if the proposal is riddled with misrepresentations until it's too late. Ask more questions and seek advice from an unrelated third party. What if the second opinion substantially confirms what was presented in the initial proposal? This may be good news. This could provide some confidence that there are strengths in the initial proposal and the business opportunity may be worth a deeper dive, or even serious consideration. What if the second opinion/competing professional advisory professional proposition varies wildly? The disparities in the proposals could prove to be a learning opportunity—giving you different perspectives. This may also be good news. The differences can provide some additional talking points that could ultimately lead to a stronger strategy. By getting a second or maybe even a third opinion on all business proposals, minor and major, you would have a peace of mind that proper due diligence was done, maybe save money on fees, and place yourself in a better position to have a successful outcome, with fewer regrets.

Unfortunately, some pro athletes don't get second opinions with business deals because they trust so easily. Even if you do thorough due diligence, the business deal may still fail. According to the U.S. Bureau of Labor Statistics (BLS), only 25% of new businesses make it to 15 years or more.[57] Proceed wisely and use all the resources available to give yourself a path forward to a good outcome.

> *"My psychiatrist told me I was crazy and I said I want a second opinion. He said, okay, you're ugly too."*
>
> —Rodney Dangerfield

Words to the wise:
Sometimes business deals are froth with misrepresentations and conflicts of interest. Know who all the players are, ask questions, and seek a second opinion. There could be some questionable self-dealings lurking in the fine print—hidden in plain sight.

Reason 14

Inexperienced Tax Preparers

> *"When you're young and you don't have a lot of business savvy, there are 2 words you forget about: FICA and sales tax."* [58]
>
> —Shaquille O'Neal

One of the most important questions to ask the person who wants to help you with your taxes is *"What are your thoughts on the jock tax?"* If the answer is "Jock tax? What's that?" walk away. You are not just an elite athlete who has made it to the big league, you are the CEO and the premier brand of an athletic and public relations enterprise. You need to take ownership of your financial reality and be an active participant in orchestrating your financial future. Tax planning is an opportunity for you to make tax-efficient and tax-saving decisions in your investment schemes.

Tax issues can be complicated, and you do not want to miss out on valuable tax-saving strategies. That's why it is imperative to thoroughly vet your professional tax team to ensure you have the most qualified professionals.

Finding a competent tax advisor/tax preparer can be tricky. Any individual who prepares a tax return or refund claims for monetary compensation is a tax preparer, but they may not be a subject matter expert. A tax preparer can also be someone not licensed or enrolled as an IRS agent but who takes compensation in return for the work done. In most states, paid tax preparers do not have to meet any standards for competence to prepare tax returns. Making general mistakes and erroneously interpreting the vast and complicated tax code are very common when preparing tax returns. Interpretations of the "right way" to present a compliant tax return can be downright subjective. The best way to start the search for a competent, qualified, and credentialed tax advisor is to ask respected friends and associates for recommendations. After you vet the individual/professional company, verify credentials and get permission to talk with existing clients of the tax professional.

Here are some questions to ask:

- Are they credentialed?
- Do they have a CPA certification?
- How long have they been in the business of tax advisory?
- Do they have experience working with professional athletes?
- Are they a member of a professional tax organization?
- Will they provide you the date and course title of the most recent continuing education (CE) classes taken?
- Do their clients routinely get audited?
- Is their tax practice audited by a governing body?
- Do they have a history of bad business practices? Does the Better Business Bureau have a file on them?

Check with the secretary of state professional licensing website and the board of accountancy to check out the CPA's record.

Not only is the professional accountant or CPA responsible for your federal tax return and numerous state tax returns, they will need to make sure all tax obligations are paid in a timely manner to keep you out of trouble with the IRS. Your tax professional should work with your financial advisor to guide you on selecting tax-efficient investments, contributing to tax qualified retirement accounts like your league's 401(k), IRAs/Roth IRAs, understanding qualified pensions, tax benefits of owning real estate, and tax-beneficial entrepreneurial ventures. Additionally, the question of which state you should be officially domiciled in is of critical importance. See Reason #38 for more information on the importance of choosing the right state domicile.

After a sports agent and your financial advisor, your tax professional is easily the next most important player on your financial team. Take the task of choosing the right tax professional very seriously. Due to the public nature of your job, pro athletes are singled out for state nonresident alien taxes, unlike other professionals. If you choose a tax "professional" who is not experienced in the professional athlete niche market and if your personal taxes are not expertly handled, you can lose a lot of money by not taking advantage of legal tax-reduction treatments and maybe even paying a boatload of back taxes. Failing to get the right tax advice is a major reason why pro athletes find themselves in financial distress. See Reason #39 for more information on the dreaded "jock tax."

You must understand the impact taxes have on your personal finances. I know it makes you weak in the knees just to think about the idea. It's critically important to get qualified tax advice on how to mitigate the vast and complicated IRS tax code and execute tax strategies to legally reduce tax liabilities to retain as much of your earnings as possible. If you get poor tax advice or if you fall behind on tax obligations, you could face some serious consequences—even jail time. Yeah, choosing the right tax professional is really important.

Here are a few things that could get you in tax hot water with the IRS:

- Unreported income,
- Under-reported income,
- Mis-reporting credits and deductions on tax returns,
- Reporting entertainment expenses, agent fees, and union dues that are no longer deductible,
- Concealing a side hustle,
- Not filing a required tax return,
- Concealing bank accounts,
- Falsified statements,
- Contributions to an unregistered foundation or charity,
- Taxable swag (gifts you received as a perk for making an appearance). Sorry, in most cases, these are actually not gifts in the eyes of the IRS, they are considered taxable income, and
- Deducting personal expenses as business expenses.

Words to the wise:
Before hiring a tax advisor/tax preparer, insist on a written letter of engagement that outlines the scope of the professional relationship and fees. Eliminate surprises.

Reason 15

Sign Here, and Here, and Here

> *"I have millions of dollars and I don't know finance. People put stuff in front of me and I signed it, and then it came back and crucified me 10 years later."*[59]
>
> —Chris Bosh, 11-time NBA All-Star

Did you know many professional sport contracts are not guaranteed? Yes, some contracts have a few clauses that state certain guarantees, but much of the language and clauses in sport contracts, signing bonuses, and endorsement deals are not guaranteed. Furthermore, many contracts can place you in the category of an at-will employee—akin to an indentured servant. Under U.S. labor law, at-will employment gives employers the legal right to dismiss or terminate an employee for any reason, at any time—as long as the reason is not illegal. Beware. Know what you are signing.

Pause for a minute: Put down this book now and ask your agent what is guaranteed in your current contract and what is not. ***Know the difference.***

Generally, sports contracts spell out very specific details on how much for how long, with the inclusion of classic perks, dispute resolution, and other provisions. Contracts play a vital role in the professional sport community, as they facilitate relationships and help enforce commitments. The agreement outlines specific actions that are required and must be taken or prohibited, making way for enforcement and remedies if either party does not perform explicit duties specified in the agreement. Contract negotiations are becoming increasingly complex and the resulting sport contracts more complicated. The process, legal jargon, and litigation concerns can be intimidating, so much so that many athletes have a fear of contracts or signing contracts. And so do I for that matter. It's scary. Your agent typically examines the documents before he presents them to you for your signature. You should thoroughly review the written terms yourself. Be sure there are no blank spaces where it appears something should be in the spaces, ask questions if you need clarifications, and check to see if your interest in the contract is agreeable before signing any contract, document, or agreement.

Never be rushed to sign a contract, and if your agent is not an attorney expert in contract law, always have an attorney or a legal review service examine the contract before you sign. It is very important that you do not sign if you do not understand the details or if the fine print is not sufficiently transparent. By having an attorney review the contract/documents before you sign, you have some assurance your interests are protected, and at the very least, you may have legal recourse against your paid attorney if you sign something that is not in your best interest or causes you financial harm.

Some contract facilitators use computer screens with check boxes that may conceal important disclosures. I hate this trend. Proceed with caution when asked to sign a document using the computer screen. Read the fine print, ask your agent to read the fine print, and request copies of everything *before* signing. Never blindly click on a box on a computer screen. If a mistake has been made, or if you signed a contract that was misrepresented, you may be able to *void* the contract. If fraud occurred, if the signature was forged, or if there was intentional misrepresentation that helped encourage the signing of the contract, then the contract is *voidable*. If you ever feel you were tricked into signing a contract, the contract may also be voidable. Examples of trickery in a contract agreement include changing out the contract details after the contract has been reviewed or a party performed some digital trickery to capture / extract / transfer your signature from a different document.

Words to the wise:

The cost of foregoing attorney review of contracts and agreements can be tenfold in comparison to what it costs to have a professional expert in contract law thoroughly review the documents before you sign. You do not have to pay thousands of dollars to a licensed attorney for this contract/document review service. There are reputable legal review services that offer this and other legal services at a fraction of the cost that a large law firm might charge.

"An ounce of prevention is worth a pound of cure."

—Benjamin Franklin

Here is a list of notable NFL players who reportedly negotiated their own sport contracts:[60]

- Lamar Jackson, QB
  - Baltimore Ravens, Extension - $42.5 MM
- Deandre Hopkins, Wide Receiver
  - Arizona Cardinals, Extension - $54.5 MM
- Richard Sherman, Cornerback
  - San Francisco 49ers- $27.5 MM
- Jacoby Brissett, QB
  - Indianapolis Colts - $30 MM
- Russell Okung, Offensive Tackle
  - Los Angeles Chargers - $53 MM
- Laremy Tunsil, Offensive Tackle
  - Houston Texans - $66 MM
- Bobby Wagner, Linebacker
  - Seattle Seahawks - $54 MM

Photo Credit: Spurs official release

Brandon signing his rookie-year contract

Reason 16

Don't Ask Questions

> *"The ability to ask questions is the greatest resource in learning the truth."*
>
> —Carl Jung, psychologist

When was the last time you changed your mobile phone service company because you noticed the charges were higher than you expected, only to sign up with another provider without asking questions about their charges? Or has this ever happened to you: You look at your most recent bank statement and notice on your debit card transaction receipt a much lower account balance than expected? You don't ask questions because it's just a few dollars different. In this age of hidden costs, inadequate transparency, financial engineering, advancing digital technologies, disintermediated blockchain capabilities, cryptocurrency, Web 3.0, metaverse, video cutting-editing-splicing, and artificial intelligence, financial services customers must become savvier about data surveillance. According to a Lexington Law survey, 36% of Americans say they review their checking account daily, while another 30% check it at least once a week.[61]

Of course, there are good reasons to keep a close eye on your banking activity. But what about your investment statements? Does it make sense to keep a watchful eye on the investment transactions and account balances? Of course it does. Some pro athletes believe themselves to be too busy to take the time to review their financial statements—perhaps naively thinking that digital systems never make mistakes. Or perhaps they trust so easily or believe they are immune to financial fraud. These are all flawed premises.

Digitization of bank and investment statements makes it easy and convenient to keep a watchful eye on your monetary transactions, but digital sophistication also makes it easier for any perpetrator with nefarious intentions to do their dastardly deeds. Following are a few reasons you should review your bank statements on a regular basis:

- Spot suspicious or unusual purchasing activities
- Catch fraudulent withdrawals or transfers
- Watch for excessive transaction fees
- Identify excessive spending
- Spot mistakes and reconcile with your recordkeeping
- See if all deposits are properly credited
- Reconcile automatic payments
- Monitor your financial health

In June 2021 LendingClub® Corporation released initial findings from its *Reality Check: Paycheck-To-Paycheck*[62] research series, conducted in partnership with PYMNTS. The report finds that 46% of Americans, as of December 2021—including individuals across a broad spectrum of income and age—are living paycheck-to-paycheck. While professional athletes may not be at risk of depleting their savings while playing for their professional teams, if they don't adopt proper account-monitoring diligence, they may one day find themselves a victim of fraud.

Investment statements, unlike bank statements, have more detailed information and seemingly pages of arcane fine print. Following is a high-level overview of what to look for on your investment account statement on a regularly basis (at least quarterly):

- Confirm name/title on the account/taxable character of the account
- Confirm advisors' names/contact information on the account
- Get comfortable with investment terminology
- Compare current total balance with previous reporting period ending balance
- Evaluate period-to-period performance

- Review account activity (transactions, deposits, withdrawals)
- Reconcile dates of cash and dividend deposits and withdrawals
- Question whether you are receiving all dividends due to you
- Look for suspicious or unusual transactions
- Monitor cash levels compared to previous reporting period statement
- Determine if you are comfortable with asset allocation
- Examine risk pie chart reference illustration
- Note fees (transactional fees and advisory management fees)

Early identification of errors, suspicious transactions, or fraudulent activity on banking and investment statements will help resolve the issue quickly and potentially identify the source of the problem more easily. If an unfamiliar, suspicious, or unauthorized transaction appears on your statement or you detect something unusual while checking your transaction details online, contact the banking/investment institution immediately to start the investigative process. Being proactive when it comes to protecting your personal information and accounts, particularly if you transact online regularly, will not only allow you to recover any funds that have been erroneously or improperly withdrawn, but will give you detection experience to help discover future transgressions.

Words to the wise:
Pay your own bills, write and sign your own checks, and have a system to audit your daily cash manager. This way you won't be surprised when you check your cash position and bank statements. *Don't delegate too much and oversee too little.*

Reason 17

No Alias

As early as middle school, some eventual professional athletes are crowned as special phenom standouts. Because of this admiration at such an early age, people with nefarious intentions start to follow them to keep track of their every move, especially regarding their personal information. The digital footprint one leaves over the years is vast and undeniable. When the phenom standout makes it to the professional stage, it becomes very easy to know a plethora of personal information about him. The moment you sign a contract with a professional sports team or a large sponsor, you are no longer a private person. Your personal credentials become known to all; we can thank the media for this. What's needed at this point—even before this point—is a personal alias (or *otherwise known as*) to shield your identity so you can have some sense of privacy.

Marilyn Monroe, a cultural icon, was a pseudonym/alias for Norma Jeane Mortenson/Norma Jeane Baker. Professional entertainers, actors, and singers change their birth names to adopt "stage names" at certain times in their professional careers, for various reasons. For the sake of privacy, pro athletes may find it beneficial and even prudent to also create an alias so their identity is obscured to the general public. Technically, you cannot legally disappear, but you can reduce your digital footprint and make it more difficult to be "known."

For strategic giggles, a pro athlete may want to adopt a stage name like other performers to help the public forget his real name, and it is perfectly legal to do so. There are many reasons they change their birth names and/or adopt an alias. Sometimes they want more credit for their accomplishments and, by giving themselves an exciting alias/nickname, the media and fans would have to mention their exciting new nickname any time their accomplishments are mentioned—giving the athletes a fun legacy that is easy to remember. Sometimes elite athletes want to honor their hero and change their birth names in remembrance of someone they hold in high regard. Some change their name to follow a new religion, to become culturally more relevant, to have a catchier, stronger, or better-sounding name, or simply because they don't like their birth name.

Identity theft and fraud are multifaceted and hard to counter, so it would serve pro athletes well to consider adopting an alias for the sake of anonymity. An alias allows you to invest in business ventures namelessly without the media's attention, to protect your mail and Amazon packages from would-be thieves, to make restaurant reservations without attracting the attention of the waitstaff, to filter online scammers, to screen email, to check in to hotels and Airbnb properties using cryptic names, to sign up for Netflix or order room service in secrecy, to give to desired or unpopular charities, to purchase real estate, cars, and other big-ticket items without the added hassle and premium upsell schemes, to open a business and/or start a partnership, to swipe right on Tinder, and even to check into an exclusive spa for much-needed rest and relaxation. You can protect yourself legally by creating a private persona that only you and a few others know. An alias is analogous to an online avatar, but stealthier.

> *"I don't know why people are so keen to put the details of their private life in public; they forget that invisibility is a superpower."*
>
> —Bansky, England-based street artist and film director whose real name and identity remain unconfirmed

Know Your Own Financial Health

Can having an alias protect your digital identity, safeguarding your financial health? Financial advisors who work with pro athletes seldom help their clients do personal credit checkups. Issues on your credit report can point to fraud and/or evidence of identity theft, and it may be hidden in plain sight. When was the last time you checked your digital identity? Your credit report? Never? This is exactly what fraud perpetrators are counting on: no personal financial accountability. Personal data like your social security number, your birthdate, your mom's maiden name, the name of your first pet, the county your middle school is located, or the instrument you played in third grade can be used by cyber criminals to open an unauthorized charge card, buy a big-ticket item, rack up medical bills, and even file a fraudulent tax return requesting a large tax refund.

Nearly half of all U.S. citizens became a victim of some form of identity theft in 2020.[63] The FTC received more than 5.7 million total fraud and identity theft reports in 2021.[64] If your personal information is breached, your financial health may be exposed for some time, as criminals can use your personal data to perpetrate identity theft long after a breach. The best way to prevent a negative cyber incident is to educate yourself and perform regular checks on your digital health, including your credit report. Knowing and protecting your digital financial identity will go a long way to help build a firewall to protect you from becoming a victim of cyber theft.

What Is a Credit Report? What Is a Credit Bureau/Agency? Why Do They Exist?

A credit report is a detailed account of your borrowing and bill-paying activities from a number of sources, including banks, financing companies, credit card companies, collection agencies, governments, and the medical community. This report is prepared by credit bureaus/agencies and is an important measure of your financial reliability, credit worthiness, and overall financial health. The report has information about how or if you pay your bills on time, your current debts, and whether you have ever filed for bankruptcy. A credit agency/credit bureau is a business that maintains historical credit information on individuals and businesses. They receive reports from lenders, bill collectors, hospitals and doctors' offices, colleges and universities, and various other sources that collect data on your paying/settlement behavior and assemble this information in a credit report.

Based on many different pieces of data in the credit report, a credit score is assigned to your financial history, known as a FICO score. Some credit information in your report carries more weight when calculating your FICO score, and unfortunately some of the data used to determine your score may not be accurate. This is the primary reason you should check your credit report on a regular basis. Ninety percent of lenders use your FICO score to help determine if you get approved for a loan.[65]

There are three major credit agencies that operate nationwide: Equifax, TransUnion, and Experian. Federal law gives you the right to receive a free copy of your credit report from each of the three national credit reporting bureaus every 12 months. To get your free report, you should not contact the three national credit bureaus individually. The only way to get your free annual credit report is by visiting the website annualcreditreport.com, calling (877) 322–8228, or completing your request by mail using the Annual Credit Report Request Form offered by the Federal Trade Commission (FTC) Consumer Information Office. You should check your credit report at least once a year, but preferably every six months, to ensure the information in your credit history is accurate and that there has not been any improper use of your personal data to secure a loan or to purchase big-ticket items. A good credit history and credit scores are vital pieces of information to maintain your overall financial well-being. Monitoring your credit history will help you understand your current credit position, audit your digital footprint, safeguard against would-be identity thieves, and stay on top of your financial health.

Fraud alert! If you feel your personal data has been compromised, you should contact one of the three credit bureaus/agencies immediately to place a fraud alert on your credit profile. Once you contact one of the agencies mentioned previously, they will inform the other two. This service shuts down inquires by new credit card companies that attempt to grant credit by someone who may not be you and protects your credit credentials. This service is free.

Words to the wise:
The internet has taken the job of secret keepers from best friends and clergy all over the world. I get this confessional stuff; it cleanses the soul. Unfortunately, sharing secrets can clean your wallet. Just know this: Once you tell someone a secret, it's no longer a secret. Profound, IKR.

Reason 18

No Budget and No Financial Accountability

Living paycheck to paycheck? CJ McCollum, NBA guard formerly with Portland Trail Blazers and now with the New Orleans Pelicans, said in an interview on the syndicated talk show *The Boardroom* that he believes an estimated 150 of the total 450 NBA players live paycheck to paycheck. Speaking on the COVID-19-fueled economic slowdown, McCollum said, "I think a lot of guys are going to be hurting, especially people on minimums or people that didn't just budget correctly and didn't expect this to happen. Maybe they loaned money or paid money to family. Maybe they're taking care of multiple people and now there's a work stoppage and for a lot of people in America."[66]

McCollum may have been talking about the current financial reality due to the pandemic economic shutdown and subsequently pay reduction around the league, but what about the status quo state of financial affairs for players who have not been in the league very long? After that interview, McCollum shared that he received some backlash, but he stood by his comments about players living paycheck to paycheck—and went on to say that he believes it's not just basketball players, but professional athletes in general, especially in their first four years in the sport. McCollum clarified, "I think there's a lot of players based on what I've seen, either mismanaged money or aren't in the position to make the right decisions financially because they're the first generation of wealth. It's hard to manage money when you've never had it before and everyone around you has never had it before."[67]

Monthly Spending Plan - Month: _____	Actual	Planned	Diff.
Housing - Mortgage / Rent			
Homeowner's Insurance / monthly			
Property Taxes / monthly			
Water, Sewer			
Electric			
Gas / Heating			
Cable / Direct TV / Netflix / Internet			
Phone / Cell Phone			
Property Maintenance, Emergency			
Lawn / Security / Other Household			
Total	$0	$0	$0
Auto			
Car Payment			
Car Insurance			
Gas / Oil Change / Maintenance			
License / Tags / Registration			
Total	$0	$0	$0
Personal			
Food, groceries / toiletries			
Dining Out / Entertainment / Fun			
Lunch @ Work			
Clothing purchases			
Hair Care / Grooming / Fitness			
Church / Charity			
Travel, vacation			
Holiday / Hobbies			
Misc., family, friends, Gifts			
Total	$0	$0	$0
Financial (outside payroll deduct)			
Healthcare Premium / Deductible			
Vision / Dental / Misc. Health			
Life Insurance Premium			
Diability / Long Term Care Insurance			
Systematic Investments			
Total	$0	$0	$0
Other Debt Payment / Expenses			
Visas, Dept Stores, Misc.			
Total Expenses	$0	$0	$0
Take Home Pay			
Side Gig			
Other Income			
Rental Income			
Investment Income			
Total Income, Net Take Home	$0	$0	$0
Difference (Income - Expenses)	$0	$0	$0

Download printable Monthly Spending Plan (MSP)
from my website. LyndaPaul.com

Does the idea of budgeting scare you? Some financial professionals call it a budget, but since that word has such a negative connotation, I adopted the phrase/term *monthly spending plan (MSP)*. One of the first things I ask my new clients to do during the onboarding process is to complete an MSP. It's just what it sounds like: a written game plan of how you expect to spend your money during the month. Your MSP is constructed using the net cash you bring in monthly (after taxes) and subtracting your expected non-discretionary expenses and then discretionary expenditures. Your MSP—how you spend your money—speaks volume about what you value and what's important to you. There are many different types of MSPs or budgets, and many ways to record your income and expenses; no one way is best. Your MSP can be a fancy, computer-generated spreadsheet with colorful graphs, or a simple plan written down on a paper drink coaster. The *how* isn't important; what matters most is that you write down what you plan to spend and work hard not to deviate from that plan.

Here are some elements your monthly spending plan should have:

✓ Expected spendable income from all sources (net of income taxes)

✓ Expenses—non-discretionary spending (necessities): basic living/food, mortgage/property taxes or rent, car payment(s), insurance, credit card payments, healthcare, prescription drugs.

✓ Savings and contributions to your emergency rainy-day fund. (Pay yourself first.) The goal is to save or allocate sufficient funds equal to one year of non-discretionary expenses.

✓ Expenses—discretionary spending: cable, Netflix, clubbing, hobbies, travel, amazon prime, luxuries, gifts to family/charity, other optional but desired expenditures

✓ Aspirational savings—big-ticket items, such as a down payment for a home, and investments

The equation: Net income − Savings − Nondiscretionary Expenses = Money remaining for discretionary spending / aspirational lifestyle.

Primary goals: To pay yourself first, spend less than you make, save for emergencies and other contingencies, and save for retirement (your future self). *Pay yourself first* is a popular phrase used in personal finance and retirement planning that encourages savers/investors to set up an automatic saving scheme to "route" money into personal savings vehicles to ensure you prioritize yourself financially before you begin paying discretionary expenses. Ideally, this automated money transfer into personal savings is done electronically on a regular basic—every pay period, signing bonus payout date, or completed endorsement deal. The ultimate game plan is financial discipline.

> *"Don't save what is left after spending but spend what is left after saving."*
>
> —Warren Buffett

Should you, a well-paid pro athlete, concern yourself with a monthly spending plan when the cash is flowing so consistently? The answer is a resounding *yes*. You are fortunate to be in the position to make very good money, and you may think the prudence of a working budget is not warranted. A monthly spending plan will give you a financial road map to understand how to wisely spend your money and identify money traps that might ensnare you, cause you to fall short of your financial goals, and derail your long-term financial security. A personalized monthly spending plan is *exactly* what you need to stay in control of your financial reality.

8 Sound Money Moves to Make in Your 20s

1. Create a budget and stick to it. Know where your money goes.
2. Find a financial mentor. Learn self-control and financial accountability.
3. Pay off debt before it become excessive and build a good credit score.
4. Understand the impact personal income taxes have on your cash flow.

5. Set up an emergency fund and investigate the different kinds of insurance.
6. Develop good money habits, pay yourself first, and spend less than you earn.
7. Secure a positive cash flow and create a second source of income if possible.
8. Start saving for retirement—for your "future self."

"He who spends more than he earns is sowing the winds of needless self-indulgence from which he is sure to reap the whirlwind of trouble and humiliation."[68]

—Richest Man in Babylon

Words to the wise:

The COVID-19 pandemic highlighted the need to have emergency savings. According to a CNBC.com online article, the majority of people were forced to dip into their rainy-day funds. Clever's Covid-19 Financial Impact Series estimated that 61% of Americans ran out of emergency savings by the end of 2020.[69] Save more, because sh*t happens.

Reason 19

What If?

The untimely passing of 24-year-old Pittsburgh Steelers quarterback Dwayne Haskins on April 9, 2022, shook the NFL, those who knew him closely, and fans around the world to their core. On the first official day of the 2022 NFL free agency signing period, Dwayne Haskins reportedly signed a $2.54 million restricted free agent tender to remain with the Pittsburgh Steelers.[70] Haskins was struck by a dump truck and killed. Stories of young, promising elite athletes dying too soon, before their pro careers end, are a sobering reminder that contingency planning must take center stage when putting together a comprehensive career and financial plan.

Early-onset CTE (chronic traumatic encephalopathy), drug overdose, alcohol-related car accidents, heart problems, and homicide are some of the ways star athletes' lives have ended too soon. Roberto Clemente (MLB), Lou Gehrig (MLB), Dale Earnhardt (NASCAR), Pat Tillman (NFL), Derrick Thomas (NFL), Reggie Lewis (NBA), Payne Stewart PGA), and most recently Bobby East (NASCAR) are just some of the many athletes who died while still active in their professional sports careers. Death is inevitable; the only question is when. No one gets out of this human experience alive. Some elite athletes and their teams of advisors don't take the time to draft a contingency plan to properly address the "what if" issues, especially the ultimate "what if" scenario. This serious oversight can have a devastating effect on your financial legacy and on family members who financially depend on you.

Careful planning is the key for pro athletes to become successful on and off the field. The career plan should be comprehensive, clear, time-defined, and goal-centered, and should include a section for contingencies, or negative unexpected circumstances, like a season-ending injury that may disrupt an otherwise-successful career. A career plan for a pro athlete might have these components:

- ✓ Skills assessment
- ✓ Position exploration
- ✓ Expected career exploration

Contingency Plan

- ✓ Action plan/training needs
- ✓ Career options in retirement

The SWOT analysis, a strategic planning tool known in the business world to identify the **S**trengths, **W**eaknesses, **O**pportunities, and **T**hreats, is used to assess a firm's situation during a business cycle and address ways to protect its economic moat. As a revenue-generating small business, you face a number of unique risks—and not all risks can be known. It makes sense you and your management team of trusted advisors do an exercise similar to a SWOT analysis to ensure all known risks are addressed in your career plans, with a few possible contingencies listed in the "what if" section.

The "T" (threats) in the SWOT analysis takes a detailed look at the risks you might face: any health, legal, or personal issue that has the potential to sideline you either for a season or for the rest of your career, rendering you unemployable. Some risks might be a body that is injury-prone or is in chronic pain, anger issues or other unaddressed mental illnesses, poor public relations behavior, legal trouble, pre-existing medical conditions, a pandemic, or being diagnosed with CTE or other career-ending injuries. As I finish this manuscript today in preparation for formatting, I am sitting at my computer happy to learn that Damar Hamlin, Safety for the Buffalo Bills is responding well to medical treatments. Hamlin went into cardiac arrest after a hit on the field during a game and had to be rushed to the hospital. Prayers for him and his family.

Professional athletes risk injury every time they train, practice, and compete. This is why many players insist on having certain clauses in their contracts to guarantee payment if they are injured. Still, this may not be enough to mitigate the financial devastation of a sports career cut short. The risk-management strategy helps either avoid, mitigate, reduce, or transfer the risk, via a contractual agreement with the team or business partners or through an insurance policy. A financial contingency plan should always accompany the comprehensive career plan.

While unpleasant, the financial impact of "what if" contingencies, including an untimely death, must be discussed. The news of NBA Legend Kobe Bryant passing away on January 26, 2020, in a helicopter crash in California, took the world by surprise and saddened the entire sport community. No one is completely prepared for an unhappy ending, but it is possible to make provisions for such an event.

> *"For everything there is a season, and a time for every matter under heaven:"*
>
> —Ecclesiastes 3:1 (ESV)

Words to the wise:
Insurance coverage provides protection against a possible eventuality; it's a delegation of risk. No one really likes the insurance gal until she arrives with a check.

Injuries happen: Darius and Lynda after his surgery

Darius en route to a championship ring with
Albany Patroons, New York

Keep your eyes on the prize

Reason 20

The Need for a Comprehensive Financial Plan

> *"Long-term thinking and planning enhance short-term decision making."*
> —Manoj Arora, *From the Rat Race to Financial Freedom*

Every decision you make will take you closer to or further away from your desired result. Decide today how you would like to live your life in the future. Do this for your future self:

1. *Visualize* and decide what you want, now and for your future self.
2. *Write down* what you want, now and for your future self.
3. *Make a simple game plan* for how to achieve your goals—and get qualified help.
4. *Work on your plan* every day.
5. *Seek accountability partners whom you can trust.*

> *"A good financial plan is a roadmap that shows us exactly how the choices we make today will affect our future."*
> —Alexa von Tobel

Uniquely, you will receive the bulk of your *lifetime* earnings over the course of a few years. These initial high-earning years have the

115

potential to lure you into a false sense of financial security. It's an inexorable truth: Making poor money moves during your peak earning years could leave you strapped for cash later in life. Financial planning for pro athletes requires a specialized approach. The challenge for professional advisors is to help you manage the early positive cash flow years while keeping you mindful that the money must reliably stretch over decades. It may not be politically correct to say, but the worst position to be in is old and broke. Money management is less about rules and more about discipline, emotion, and psychological mindfulness. The toughest challenges your financial advisor has by far are to encourage you to spend less now and to create a sound plan to help you manage three to eight years of earnings to last a lifetime—and potentially provide an avenue for generational wealth.

A comprehensive financial plan helps you define short-term and long-term financial goals, pinpoint lifestyle aspirations that are most important to you, identify roadblocks that can get in the way of you achieving your goals, and summarize ways to mitigate financial risks. A comprehensive financial plan should be relatively simply and consist of six areas:

1. Your current financial position
2. Risk management/protection planning
3. Wealth creation/accumulation/investments
4. Tax planning
5. Retirement planning
6. Estate and legacy planning

Note: The One-Page Planner™ at the end of this section shows how to construct a basic comprehensive plan.

The following list of considerations is not all-inclusive.

Your Current Financial Position
- Income/expenses
- Cash flow management
- Cash reserve levels
- Cash reserve strategies

- Debt management
- Net worth statement

Risk Management/Protection Planning
- Property and casualty insurance/auto and home insurance/umbrella insurance
- Disability insurance
- Life insurance
- Long-term care insurance
- Medical/health insurance
- Pet insurance
- Beneficiary designations
- Special needs
- Alternative insurance coverage
- Prenuptial agreements
- Kidnap, ransom, and extortion insurance

Wealth Creation/Accumulation/Investments
- Investment risk tolerance
- Financial investing literacy
- Asset allocation
- The Rule of 72/dollar cost averaging
- Diversification strategies
- Time frame
- Tax character of investments
- Investment fees

Tax Planning
- Federal taxes
- State domicile
- State taxes
- "Jock tax"
- Local/county taxes
- Tax-efficient strategies

- Tax-reduction strategies
- Tax-deferred investing
- Tax-free investing
- Tax diversification
- Tax-loss harvesting
- Qualified and non-qualified investment vehicles
- Tax considerations of business ownership
- Tax character of investments
- Entrepreneurships/business entity declaration
- Investment property
- 1035/1031 exchanges

Retirement Planning
- Retirement income needs
- Relocation/downsizing
- Lifestyle changes
- Emotional transition
- 401(k)s/Traditional IRAs/Roth IRAs/Roth conversion
- Accumulation/distributions
- Pre-59½ distributions
- Required minimum distributions (RMD) at age 73
- Employer pensions/annuity income
- Social Security (eligibility and claiming time frame)
- Healthcare/long-term care
- Medicare/supplement and Medigap insurance
- 11 key risks in retirement contingency planning

Estate and Legacy Planning
- Will/trust/power of attorney/healthcare directives
- Asset ownership/how titled
- Property ownership/how titled
- Succession planning / Buy-Sell Agreements
- Minor children/special needs dependents
- Beneficiaries/contingent beneficiaries
- Generation skipping

- Estate balancing/equalization
- Provision for spendthrift beneficiaries
- Estate liquidation
- Estate taxes

Words to the wise:
Get started now. Take time this week to provide commentary to the lists above and use your notes as a framework to put together a rough draft of your comprehensive plan. Then engage with a CFP® professional to co-create a suitable financial game plan. Your future self will praise you again and again for your foresight.

> *"If you fail to plan, you are planning to fail."*
> —Benjamin Franklin

6 Areas of Financial Planning
The One-Page Planner™ (Basic)

Will / Trust / Power of Attorney & Healthcare Directives

Legacy Planning
Charitable Gifting

Guaranteed Lifetime Income

ESTATE PLANNING

401(k) Contributions
Traditional IRA / Roth IRA
Qualified Plans / Pensions
Tax-Deferred Annuities

RETIREMENT PLANNING

529 College Savings Plan
Tax-Efficient Investments
Real Estate Investments

TAX PLANNING

Investments
Self-Employment
Business Creation

WEALTH ACCUMULATION

Life Insurance / LTC
Disability Insurance
Car / Home Ins.

RISK MANAGEMENT

Monthly Spending Plan
Cash Flow / Debts /
Credit Cards /

Net Worth Statement

FINANCIAL POSITION

Emergency Funds

Lynda Paul, CFP® Certified Financial Planner™ (210) 467-5113

www.SoundMoneySanAntonio.com

Visit my website to download the One-Page Planner™ to start your comprehensive plan. LyndaPaul.com

120

CHAPTER 3

Dealing with Self and
the Entrepreneurial Spirit

You've Earned It!

As the purveyor of your professional brand, you must ensure you are in tip-top physical condition to compete at the highest level. The same is true about your mental preparedness and business acumen. This chapter is about the importance of investing in your brain as well as other aspects of your mental well-being to advance your professional brand and financial prowess. Your body is your physical capital, and your brain is your intellectual capital. According to research, successful pro athletes possess three states of readiness as they train for peak performance: technical know-how, physical ability, and mental malleability. All three ready states are important in your sport career, but if you are to excel in managing your personal finances and creating lifestyle-sustaining wealth, the mental game and keeping your brain tenaciously malleable are critically important and will serve you well. Wealth is created or destroyed based on what we put in our brains or fail to put in our brains, and how well we manage our behavior. Proactively getting ready to handle tough, big-boy game-time issues is the same mental process needed to develop the mindset to create and maintain a sound financial gameplan.

Once you master the tools needed to have a successful business presence, making the right money moves will become second nature. If you stay ready, you never have to get ready. This is true in all aspects of your personal, financial, and professional life. If you neglect to take control of these important facets of your life, you risk a shortened professional career and can be ill-prepared financially for the future. Keep the brain healthy by constantly investing in its expansive growth, making sound judgment calls when dealing with business matters, taking a calculated approach with giving and lending money, accepting full responsibility for your financial health, trusting your instincts, and understanding the holy grail of making money grow: compound interest.

> *"Compound interest is the eighth wonder of the world. He who understands it, earns it. He who doesn't, pays it."*
>
> —Albert Einstein

Reason 21

The Brain = Intellectual Capital

Pro athletes are intellectual people. They have a good grasp of physics and understand how body mechanics affect their performance. They learn and memorize complicated plays and strategic formations to maximize the potential for success. They understand how power, strength, and speed translate to better performance. They learn to master poise under stress to ensure a constant state of readiness. The elite athlete's brain accumulates knowledge, teaches itself specific skills through practice, develops thought-management techniques that generate energy to drive actions, cultivates problem-solving capabilities, and creates new ideas. The brain constantly improves its users' communication qualities, develops solid leadership credentials with experiential engagements, and enhances relatability and relational skills with every human interaction. The brain possesses all the circuitry needed to master most tasks and keep itself efficiently operational for your entire life. You would agree that you are carrying around a very powerful and valuable piece of equipment, yes?

When we think about an asset (a resource with value), most of us think about a financial asset—something we can invest money into to achieve a profit. From this perspective, the brain—a non-financial entity—is the most important asset you have and the most beneficial, most profitable, and most fruitful asset to invest in. We think of the brain as a tool, not an asset. The brain's capacity to think, to feel, to perceive, and to induce action should be seen as more than a tool. The brain is a complex organ that controls thoughts, memory, emotion, touch, motor skills, vision, breathing, temperature, hunger, and every process that regulates our body.[71] With these positive attributes, the brain is more valuable than any real estate holding or stock portfolio that exists in the world. Its full capacity is unknown by man. The brain

MAKING SOUND MONEY MOVES

is our MVA (most valuable asset), so any investment in the brain will yield a spectacularly positive return on that investment, increasing its value multifold. Once value, in the form knowledge or neurological connections, is seized by the brain, it never loses that value. Unlike real estate or stock, to which the value is assigned by a third party and can fluctuate, the brain's value never diminishes and is lifelong.

> *"The mind, once stretched by a new idea, never returns to its original dimensions."*
>
> —Ralph Waldo Emerson

How much *time* have *you* invested in the health and expansion of your brain to increase its value? How much *money* have you invested in your brain to increase its value? Your financial outcome will be greatly improved if you treat your brain as an asset. Boost your intellectual capital by reading financial literature, ingesting trustworthy financial commentary, observing and emulating sound money practices, and asking questions. As a byproduct of improving your intellectual capital, you will reduce the amount of money lost from poor decision-making.

Words to the wise:
Set aside Cryptocurrency, NFTs, Bitcoin, Ethereum, stocks, bonds, mutual funds, and ETFs. Your brain is your most valuable asset. Invest in your brain first, then you will know better how to invest in the other assets to grow your net worth.

Reason 22

This Time It's Different

If you aren't already, soon you will be inundated with requests to engage in business ventures by friends, family members, and associates. It's exciting to brainstorm new business ideas and chat about what's trending with people whose company you enjoy. Going into business with a good friend or with someone you've known since childhood *may* alleviate some of the stress that comes with starting a new business venture with strangers. Who better to share a very special business journey with than a good friend, your wingman, or a beloved family member?

A word of caution: Whether you've known this potential business partner for decades or been friends for only a few months, going into business with a friend is just as risky as partnering with a stranger. In some ways, it may be more troublesome. You don't really know someone until you've worked with them on a regular basis. It is likely, once you're in business with a friend or family member, the experience will change your relationship. If you are not mindful of sound business judgment and if you abandon critical due diligence in researching business ventures, you can end up losing your money *and* the relationship. Research all business ventures and thoroughly vet potential business partners before signing on the dotted line.

Here are some things to think about if you are considering partnering up for a business venture:

- ✓ Know your business partner. Take an objective look at their current work ethics, their business history, their resume, and what they bring to the table.
- ✓ Be professional. Remove the fun equation until after the work is done, stay focused on the business, and, when there are

friendly disagreements, be objective and keep emotions at a minimum.

✓ Agree on business roles and respective responsibilities from the beginning. You should have separate business duties based on the strengths that each of you bring to the partnership. Also, if one of you is vacationing, sick, or otherwise incapacitated, a contingency or business continuity plan should be put in writing.

✓ Put everything in writing. The best way to protect yourself, your invested capital, and your friendship is to put everything in writing. The business plan, funding sources, salaries, bonus payout calculations / timelines, vacation schedules, business loans, profit distribution percentages, and even dissolution or exit arrangements should all be in writing.

✓ Communicate often and don't intermingle your personal and business lives.

Marketing Research

Seek counsel from a marketing research consultant before agreeing to go into business with a friend, an associate, an established firm, or *any* entity, even if you decide to go it alone. Forward-thinking marketing research consultants *identify* a niche in which the new business can innovate and excel, *maintain* an open dialogue to build trust and rapport, and *provide* actionable insights. They are true partners who ask relevant questions with the client's business objectives in mind, then help deliver the goods.

There are many reasons businesses fail: money runs out, an inability to obtain financing, failure to get traction for the product or services offered, bad partnership/toxic relationships, theft, and poor marketing. A top reason cited by entrepreneurs for their business failure is poor marketing research.[72] They just didn't know what they didn't know. It's true a very high percentage of new companies/business ventures fail within the first five years, but a respectable number of businesses succeed. Case in point: At the time of the printing of this book, I will be celebrating 28 years as an entrepreneur. I left my comfortable accounting position at Abbott

Laboratories in 1995 to start the journey to open my financial planning business, Sound Money Management, INC.

Words to the wise:
Three of the businesses and investment opportunities that receive the most interest from pro athletes are restaurants/nightclubs, car dealerships, and a personal shoe line/clothing line. All are notoriously poor investment ideas because they all require a repetitive infusion of capital and are labor-intensive. Additionally, the profit margins are spectacularly thin. These all sound very glamorous. I get it. Caution: Unless your name is MJ, if you are ever approached by an advisor or investor who wants you to invest in any of the previously mentioned business ventures, don't do it. You will probably be assured that "This new concept is fail-proof with no downside risks" or hear something like "This time it will be different." Run. Away.

> *"The four most dangerous words in investing are: 'this time it's different'."*
>
> —Sir John Templeton

Reason 23

Merci Beaucoup

You love to give. Science confirms this, as research shows that giving to others genuinely makes people happier.[73] It's well documented in the media that professional athletes are generous: donating to charities, taking their families out of unsafe neighborhoods, paying the medical bills of a fan who has been stricken with cancer, paying total education costs for a segment of impoverished students, paying off college student-loan debts, even building schools for economically disadvantaged youths. Many pro athletes set up foundations and charities so they can encourage those in need to ask for assistance (and consequently making it easier to receive the tax deductions that they are entitled to for their generosity). Elite athletes realize they live a privileged life and are very conscious of how important it is to give back to those who are less fortunate. The internet is inundated with stories of pro athletes who make charitable contributions, including generous donations made in 2020 to support those in need during the global pandemic.

Tennis megastar Serena Williams, who has won 23 Grand Slam singles titles, the most by any player in the Open Era, is touted as one of the most charitable athletes in the world.[74] She is actively involved in a variety of worthy causes, including the education of children in Asia in her role as the Goodwill Ambassador for UNICEF. She also founded the Serena Williams Foundation, which focuses on education, helping kids from low-income families to enroll in college, with funds also paying for legal aid for people at the poverty level. Through her foundation, Serena's generosity has provided funding for immunization programs in Ghana and schools in Kenya, as well as support for the Elton John Aids Foundation, the Big Brothers Big Sisters program, Hearts of Gold, and much more.

Along the same lines of giving to charities from a generous heart, professional athletes are also asked to be bank and lender of choice for family members, friends, and associates—sharing their savings with people they love. Generosity, however, has limits. Have you ever been in the awkward position of being asked by a family member for a loan? Have you had a sneaky feeling you will never see the loan repaid? When a good friend or a family member in need asks for a loan or a financial favor, it's only natural to want to help them out. But should you?

The benefit of your family member or friend asking you for a loan is obvious: The borrower is able to *bypass* the need to complete an application that would be required by an unsympathetic financial institution, *dodge* the need to explain poor credit history and a low credit score, *skip out on* presenting collateral to secure the loan, *escape* the payment of all lending fees, and *forgo* the anguish and worry about paying interest that would have been charged by a bank. Additionally, on top of all these perks, paying back the loan may even be optional. It makes sense for your friends to ask you for a loan, instead of seeking funds from a traditional lender. Before you say yes, ask yourself: *Does it make sense for me to lend money without accountability?*

Are you being a good steward of your hard-earned money? As someone eager to please and show loyalty to family and friends, your mental state might make you more vulnerable, thereby putting pressure on your heart strings to give out more loans than what is otherwise prudent. The harm comes when your generosity causes you to overcommit your financial resources. This is a sure way to find yourself on the road to financial insolvency.

Words to the wise:
Don't give until it hurts.

Reason 24

Emotional Immaturity

The American Psychological Association (APA) defines *emotional maturity* as "a high and appropriate level of emotional control and expression."[75] These are key characteristics of someone who is emotionally mature:

- They take responsibility for their behavior and don't blame others when things don't go as planned.
- They show empathy and try to do as much good for others as they can.
- They own their mistakes. They know how to apologize when they have done someone wrong and find ways to rectify the situation. The emotionally mature person also does not have the desire to be right all the time and acknowledges that they may not have all the answers.
- They show vulnerability. The emotionally mature are willing to share their own struggle.

A person who is emotionally immature lacks the above characteristics and other social skills. They are known to "act out" and use inappropriate behavior, including poor spending behavior, as a form of escapism to cope with life's pressures. Some behaviors of an emotionally immature person include impulsive behavior, demanding attention, bullying, avoidance (poor sense of the future), and narcissism. Immature people appear to care only about themselves. They dislike compromise and don't want to take other people's ideas into consideration. They always want to have their own way.[76]

Pro athletes who take responsibility for their actions show integrity, character, and respect for others. Some young elite athletes, due primarily to their age and grooming, were never required to take responsibility for their bad behavior. They may have been bailed out of trouble, protected from law enforcement and other authorities, or shielded from media attention, and they generally led a nonstick, Teflon existence before becoming a professional athlete. The expectation for personal accountability changes once an elite athlete enters professional sports. Many pro athletes make more money selling their brand off the playing field than they do from their professional salaries. These lucrative deals can quickly be in jeopardy if the pro athlete damages his brand by bad behavior. Following are a few well-known athletes who lost endorsement deals because of poor and often-illegal behaviors: [77]

- Lance Armstrong, suspected use of banned substances
    Estimated $150 million lost
- Tiger Woods, highly publicized extramarital affairs
    Estimated $22 million lost
- Maria Sharapova, failed drug test
    Estimated $ lost unknown
- Michael Vick, running an illegal dogfighting ring
    Estimated $ lost unknown
- Ray Rice, allegedly knocking his fiancée unconscious
    Estimated $2 million lost per year
- Michael Phelps, picture of him allegedly smoking pot
    Estimated $ lost unknown
- Gilbert Arenas, pleaded guilty/unregistered firearms
    Estimated $40 million lost

With public surveillance and security cameras lurking around every corner, cell phone paparazzi, and social media vigilance technology, it's a wonder that more pro athletes are not outed for bad behavior. Emotional immaturity hurts and can be very costly. Own it. Bad behavior can damage personal relationships, is harmful to your professional brand, and can choke your ability to attract lucrative endorsement deals.

Words to the wise:
Emotional immaturity invites poor decisions. Keep a low profile and be on your best behavior while in public to maximize your earning potential over your abbreviated sports career.

Reason 25

Instincts

It's contract negotiation time. You have a tough decision to make and the powers that be are expecting your answer soon. Because of an eleventh-hour addition to the contract, you and your agent have very little information about the future value of the added provision. Pressure is on. They need your response by 3 p.m. today, or the contract is null and void. Anxiety is creeping in; you are spectacularly concerned about the consequences of a bad decision. Exhale. You got this! You know stuff, and you know you know stuff. You trust yourself. You are a good listener and a good learner, and you have opinions. You read often and know how to turn knowledge into understanding. You are consciously aware of the pros and cons of most situations, regularly challenge the status quo, and are sufficiently skeptical. You know when something feels good or bad, right or wrong, fake or genuine, and most of all you can sniff out bullshit a mile away. You're logical, enterprising, self-reliant with high self-esteem, and realistic. Some might even call you conventional. You are adept at hearing what is unsaid and asking relevant questions. You are genetically hard-wired to cope with uncertainties, and you already possess good "instincts" and intuitive abilities, or gut feelings, to make a proper decision in a situation like this, even without relevant data and analytics.

Intuition is a knowing. Listen to it. Trust it. Instincts are gifts from God, and when combined with prayers for guidance, you have a match made in heaven, making a good outcome almost inevitable. I repeat: You got this. To uplevel your decision-making abilities, you need good judgment. Exercising good judgment often means thinking critically about issues, using analytical skills and the ability to recognize patterns, and listening to others' opinions before deciding.

You are surrounded by well-intentioned family members, advisors, coaches, teammates, and intrusive fans—all eager to provide their opinions on the best career, business, or financial moves you should make. With so much unsolicited advice coming in from so many people with conflicting viewpoints, how can you discern whose opinion you should listen to? All your life you've had people make decisions for you. Now that you are in the pros, the need to make decisions, especially sound money-management decisions, has escalated in importance, with life-altering consequences.

If the quality of good judgment is the ability to combine personal characteristics with relevant knowledge and experience to form opinions, you are only lacking one important element: experience. The more real-life exposure you get, the more you will expand your experience. It will take intentionality and practice to add to your decision-making experience. Quiet the noise in your head so you can pay attention to the relevant inner messages, collect data, feel the emotions, connect with others by asking good questions and expecting good answers, and pay attention to the nonverbal and your environment. Like fine wine, decision-making skills get better with time.

"Intuition and instinct kept us humans safe for thousands of years, but as we've evolved over the ages, we've learned to lean on data, learned responses, other people's opinions, and third-party education to make decisions—rendering our gut instincts impotent," says Dr. Tasha Holland-Kornegay, founder of Wellness is Real Life.[78] But this does not have to be your story. Don't abandon your judgment. Over your professional journey and your life after sports, you will need to trust your instinct. You got this.

> *"Never discredit your gut instinct. You are not paranoid. Your body can pick up on bad vibrations. If something deep inside of you says something is not right about a person or situation, trust it."*[79]
>
> —Lynda Paul, author and financial advisor

Words to the wise:
Perfect can be the enemy of good. Don't take your eyes off the prize by striving to make the perfect decision. Perfection eludes. A good decision will bring about a good outcome.

Reason 26

The Power of Compound Interest: The Rule of 72

Compound Interest

Financial professionals around the globe educate clients on the idea that if you put money in an interest-bearing account with a financial institution, like a bank, your savings will grow without you having to add additional money to the account. How does money "miraculously" grow? Interest. In the context of this segment, interest is payment *from* a deposit-taking financial institution given *to* a depositor for the opportunity to use the funds. It is usually reflected as an annual percentage. In layman terms, as a depositor, you earn interest on your deposited amount (principal) just by storing your funds with a financial institution and allowing them to use your funds (borrow) for their business needs. There are two kinds of interest: simple and compound.

Simple interest – The amount you earn on the money you originally deposited (your principal) expressed as an annual percentage rate -e.g., 3% per year. As your funds sit in your account, interest accumulates over time – based on your original principal amount and the interest rate offered by the financial institution.

Compound interest – The amount you earn on the money you originally deposited **and** the amount you earn on any previous interest that has accumulated in your account. Interest is generated and paid on **both**, the original principal deposited, and the interest already earned and accumulated in the account. Compound interest allows your money to grow faster than with simple interest. The compounding effect is a game changer. It's referred to as the "eighth wonder of the world" in economic circles.

Let's say you have $1,000 saved in your account (your principal) and it earns 6% simple interest rate of return for the year. At the end of the first year, you would have earned interest totaling $60. Let's do the math: $1,000 x .06 = $60 interest earned. At the end of year one, your account balance would be $1,000 (original principal) + $60 (simple interest) = $1,060.00 (total balance)

Shortcut: $1,000.00 x 1.06 = $1,060.00

In year two, if you do not withdraw any money from this account or add any additional funds, and the financial institution is paying a 6% annual interest rate, again you will earn interest on the original principal of $1,000 = $60. Now, your year-end balance will be:

$1,060.00 (beg balance) + $60.00 (new interest) = $1,120.00 (new balance). Simple interest.

In the case of compound interest, in year 2, you earn interest on your original principal *and* interest on the interest you earned in year 1. Let's do the math:

Shortcut: $1,060.00 x 1.06 = $1,123.60

In year three, if you do not withdraw any money from this account, or add any additional funds, you can now earn interest on the original principal of $1,000, earn interest on the year-one interest earned of $60, *and* earn interest on the year-two interest earned of $63.60.

Let's do the math:

Shortcut: $1,123.60 x 1.06 = $1,191.02

As you can see, with just $1,000 principal deposited into an account, interest is continuously earned on the principal *and* on the interest earned in the previous periods. This is the beautiful financial concept of compounding interest. It's magical! The real magic is if you can resist the temptation to perform the disappearing act, and keep your hands off the money in your account so it can benefit from compounding interest.

The Rule of 72

Want to buy a home and you need to save big money? Need to double the amount in your savings account? How long will it take to 2X your money, using the "magical" powers of compounding interest? The Rule of 72 is a quick, useful formula used in the financial world to estimate the number of years required to double an investment at a given annual rate of return. Don't be intimidated by the math; just follow the flow and learn this very important personal finance lesson about how compound interest works. By dividing 72 by the annual rate of return, an investor can obtain a rough estimate of how many years it will take for the initial investment to double.

$i =$ the expected rate of return annually (6%)

$t =$ the time in years it will take to double the money.

$$t = \frac{72}{i} \qquad t = \frac{72}{6} \longrightarrow t = 12 \text{ years}$$

If you place money in an account that you project will earn 6% every year, you can expect your money to double every 12 years. Let's say you are 22 years old in 2023 and you make a one-time investment of $5,000 in an account that you expect to earn 6% per year without adding more money to the account. Based on the Rule of 72, the $5,000 investment will double every 12 years. Let's do the math:

Rule of 72 Results Using $5,000
June 2023, year one starts (age 22) $ 5,000
June 2035, 12 years later (age 34) $10,000
June 2047, 12 years later (age 46) $20,000
June 2059, 12 years later (age 58) $40,000
June 2071, 12 years later (age 70) $80,000

Using the same equation, instead of $5,000, what if you take half of your bonus check—say, $50,000—and set it aside for your retirement instead of spending it on another trip to Las Vegas with your friends? Or weekly VIP Bottle Service? Based on the illustrated Rule of 72, this $50,000 could grow from the magic of compounding interest by doubling every 12 years to **$800,000.** What a difference it makes when you add a zero. It all adds up! If you keep the money in the account and never withdraw the funds, at retirement you can expect to see a substantial accumulated savings amount based on compound interest/rate of return on investments. Steady, smart growth.

Rule of 72 Results Using $50,000
June 2023, year one starts (age 22) $ 50,000
June 2035, 12 years later (age 34) $100,000
June 2047, 12 years later (age 46) $200,000
June 2059, 12 years later (age 58) $400,000
June 2071, 12 years later (age 70) $800,000

Note: These are hypothetical illustrations. Very few investment vehicles pay a linear rate-of-return every year. Generally, rates of return on investments fluctuate from period to period, or even daily. These illustrations simply show conceptually how compound interest works and how money/wealth grows over time. Your risk tolerance will impact your expected rate of return.

Using the Rule of 72, instead of investing $5,000 or $50,000, what if you spent your entire signing bonus on a trip to Mykonos with 10 of your closest friends on your 22nd birthday and you have $0 dollars to invest? Let's do the math:

Rule of 72 Results Using $0
June 2023, year one starts (age 22) $0
June 2035, 12 years later (age 34) $0
June 2047, 12 years later (age 46) $0
June 2059, 12 year later   (age 58) $0
June 2071, 12 years later (age 70) $0

Rule of 72 Tested - Tax-deferred Growth at 6% Per Year
Let's Do The Math

Earnings at 6% - doubles ever 12 years

$	50,000.00		
	6.00%	$ 3,000.00	
Less: Fed Taxes 20%		$ -	
Jan-24	$ 53,000.00		Year 1 Ending Balance
Beginning Balance	$ 53,000.00		
	6.00%	$ 3,180.00	
Less: Fed Taxes 20%		$ -	
Jan-25	$ 56,180.00		Year 2 Ending Balance
Beginning Balance	$ 56,180.00		
	6.00%	$ 3,370.80	
Less: Fed Taxes 20%		$ -	
Jan-26	$ 59,550.80		Year 3 Ending Balance
Beginning Balance	$ 59,550.80		
	6.00%	$ 3,573.05	
Less: Fed Taxes 20%		$ -	
Jan-27	$ 63,123.85		Year 4 Ending Balance
Beginning Balance	$ 63,123.85		
	6.00%	$ 3,787.43	
Less: Fed Taxes 20%		$ -	
Jan-28	$ 66,911.28		Year 5 Ending Balance
Beginning Balance	$ 66,911.28		
	6.00%	$ 4,014.68	
Less: Fed Taxes 20%		$ -	
Jan-25	$ 70,925.96		Year 6 Ending Balance

Year 7 Beginning Balance	$ 70,925.96		
	6.00%	$ 4,255.56	
Less: Fed Taxes 20%		$ -	
Jan-26	$ 75,181.51		Year 7 Ending Balance
Beginning Balance	$ 75,181.51		
	6.00%	$ 4,510.89	
Less: Fed Taxes 20%		$ -	
Jan-27	$ 79,692.40		Year 8 Ending Balance
Beginning Balance	$ 79,692.40		
	6.00%	$ 4,781.54	
Less: Fed Taxes 20%		$ -	
Jan-28	$ 84,473.95		Year 9 Ending Balance
Beginning Balance	$ 84,473.95		
	6.00%	$ 5,068.44	
Less: Fed Taxes 20%		$ -	
Jan-25	$ 89,542.38		Year 10 Ending Balance
Beginning Balance	$ 89,542.38		
	6.00%	$ 5,372.54	
Less: Fed Taxes 20%		$ -	
Jan-26	$ 94,914.93		Year 11 Ending Balance
Beginning Balance	$ 94,914.93		
	6.00%	$ 5,694.90	
Less: Fed Taxes 20%		$ -	
Jan-27	$ 100,609.82		Year 12 Ending Balance

> *"The best time to plant a tree was 20 years ago.*
> *The second best time is now."*
>
> —Chinese proverb

Words to the wise:

Don't underestimate the compounding effects of sound money moves, no matter how small. It will take discipline and patience, but you will be rewarded. Take good care of your financial resources, and your financial resources will take good care of you.

Start while you are young, and watch your money grow over time.

Visit my website to do an asset growth illustration.

LyndaPaul.com

Reason 27

Creating Wealth

Wealth is an abundance of valuable possessions, money, or economic resources. Building wealth means accumulating these valuable economic resources. Everyone talks about investing money when they discuss the idea of building wealth. Without a doubt investing is an important part of financial planning and sound money management, but there's more to creating and building wealth than investing money. Economic assets are resources with economic value that are **owned** by an individual. Liabilities are debts or something that are **owed** and must be repaid.

Assets Owned – Liabilities Owed = Net Worth

Net worth is the most used measure of wealth, determined by taking the economic assets you own and subtracting the liabilities you owe. The name of the wealth-accumulation game is increasing your net worth. Your net worth represents where you are financially at a particular moment in time, and it usually fluctuates over time.

The calculation is straightforward, and the resulting figure can be very useful at a given point in time. But the real value comes from doing this net worth calculation on a regular basis—to track your financial score over time and to evaluate your progress.

In simple terms, there are only two ways to grow your net worth: increase the assets you own or decrease the liabilities you owe. Growing your net worth starts with a financial game plan and a wealth-building mindset; success depends on financial discipline. A portfolio

144

of diversified, appreciating stocks and income-paying bonds is a great way to create wealth. Building a portfolio of investment real estate property might be a better way to build wealth that lasts for generations. Property depreciation and like-kind exchanges under IRC Section 1031 are economic game changers. On the flip side of building wealth, many athletes are not sufficiently knowledgeable about the many ways net worth can erode over time. Compulsive and unchecked spending, runaway child-support payments, and legal trouble can substantially deplete net worth. Being an early adopter of and influencer to unvetted digital currency schemes can also substantially reduce your net worth.

How to create a w-e-a-l-t-h mindset? By using this convenient acronym by TradingWalk[80]:

W—Write down what you want. Pay yourself first

E—Envision your future. Make money on your money.

A—Affirm your desire.

L—Listen to your inner voice.

T—Take action and transform.

H—Hold the vision.

Creating wealth, building and expanding wealth, protecting and preserving wealth—all worthwhile endeavors that take time and intentionality. While compound interest is a significant part of building wealth, there are other parts to building and creating wealth that you will need to master, over time.

Words to the wise:
The net worth statement is how I keep score of my clients' progress. If your calculated net worth is increasing over time, you are winning. If it is decreasing, then adjustments are needed. In the money game, you win by not losing.

Net Worth Worksheet	Sound Money Management – Year 2023

Liquid Assets

Cash & Cash Equivalents (checking, savings, CDs, etc.)	$_____
Vehicles, Furniture and Other Personal Property	$_____
Taxable Investments Account (Individual, Joint, Trusts)	$_____
Individual Retirement Accounts (IRA, SEP, Roth, etc.)	$_____
Retirement Plan Accounts (401(k), 403(b), 457, etc.)	$_____
Annuities (non-qualified - not included above)	$_____
Employee Stock Options, Shares of Stock held in certificate form	$_____
Fine Jewelry, Art, Collectibles, Digital Currencies, NFTs, etc.	$_____
Total Liquid Assets	$_____

Non-Liquid Assets

Primary Residence (FMV)	$_____
Secondary Residence / Investment Properties	$_____
Business Ownerships / Investments	$_____
Other (specify: _____)	$_____
Total Non-Liquid Assets	$_____
Total Liquid and Non-Liquid Assets	$_____

Liabilities

Primary Residence Mortgage	$_____
Other Property Mortgages / Second Lien	$_____
Personal / Business Loans (Secured Debts)	$_____
Student Loans / Personal Loans (Unsecured)	$_____
Credit Cards / Installment Loans / Unsecured Debt	$_____
Other (specify: _____)	$_____
Total Liabilities	$_____

Net Worth (Total Assets Less Total Liabilities)	$_____

Advisor: Lynda Paul, CFP®   **(210) 467-5113**

Go to my website to download a printable net worth worksheet and sample net worth statement.

LyndaPaul.com

CHAPTER 4

The Entourage, Entertainment, Consumptive Behaviors, and Dopamine

Epicurean

People all over the world have opinions on how you should behave—and these opinions vary and often contradict. Seems funny that many think you're doing *you* all wrong. If you scroll through social media, you will undoubtedly find someone commenting on something you said or did—good or bad. You are judged for every decision you make on and off the field/court/ice, and your behavior is often the talk of the town—and for good reason. You are an influencer. Pro athletes are known for their extravagant lifestyles and seemingly insatiable appetite for the best this world has to offer. They pursue pleasure with epicurean zeal and purchase aspirational things like luxury cars, expansive homes, extravagant designer clothes, flashy jewelry, and they are sometimes generous to a fault. Yeah—y'all extra. If over-the-top spending behaviors are not corralled, they can get out of control and seduce you into living a life beyond your means, leading to financial ruin.

A substantial portion of your spending may be gleefully directed toward your friends and entourage, a cadre of the usual suspects. Everyone acknowledges members of the pro athlete's entourage serve important roles to help him stay grounded and focused. It has been well documented that the people with whom you surround yourself will ultimately become your support system and will have an important role in your successes and failures.

Who ya wit? (in my Bernie Mac voice)

Massive Entourages of Former and
Current Pro Athletes (Estimates)

Manny Pacquiao, former pro boxer—100+ members[81]

Allen Iverson, former NBA guard—rumored to have at least 50 members[82]

LeBron James, current NBA star—50+ members[83]

Andre Rison, former NFL wide receiver—40-person entourage[84]

Mike Tyson, former pro boxer—rumored to have 200+ members at one time[85]

Floyd Mayweather, Jr., boxer—dozens of members in his entourage affectionately was once known as the original "Money Team"[86]

Let's do the math: You have an entourage of 30 people. You pay for 30 flights, 30 hotel rooms, ground transportation, meals, and whatever else. During the season your entourage expenditures can escalate. The same applies to the off-season if your peeps are full-time attendants or they do not have a paying gig during the time you are off the grid. Every time I read about the classic case when NBA star Allen Iverson being "extra" and exhibiting poor financial decision-making reportedly landed at the airport and forgot where his car was parked, I moan in disbelief. He abandoned his search for his car, called a cab, then famously went to a nearby car dealership to purchase a new car.

Interesting Purchases by Pro Athletes[87]

Pro golfer Tiger Woods reportedly spent $40 million on property in Florida, razed the old mansion that was on the property, then spent upward of $20 million to build his lavish mansion and private golf course, which is situated on 10 acres of oceanfront. Total: $60 million dollars.

Pro boxer Mike Tyson reportedly spent $4.5 million on cars and motorbikes, $2.2 million on a gold bathtub as a gift, $400,000 per month on lifestyle and miscellaneous expenses, $140,000 on three Bengal tigers plus $140,000 for annual food/housing/maintenance, and $125,000 per year for an animal trainer to take care of the big cats. Total: $10 million dollars.

Pro boxer Floyd Mayweather, Jr. reportedly spent $10 million on an engagement ring. Mayweather stated the ring was made of 25-carat fancy intense yellow diamonds. The ring also had a matching bracelet made of 50-carat diamonds that costs an additional $6 million. They never married. Total: $16 million dollars.

This Chapter Attempts to Shed Light on These Two Questions:

1. Why are professional athletes so extra?
2. Why do they appear to always want more?

More victories, more accolades,
more love interests, more stuff.

Is **dopamine** the culprit? Dopamine is a neurotransmitter, a chemical produced in our bodies that drives us to seek and repeat pleasurable activities. It makes us feel good. The higher level of dopamine we have, the more we are motivated to do a thing. Elite athletes often have heightened levels of dopamine due to diet and training; this may be an evolutionary by-product of the male athlete. Dopamine increases the athlete's attention toward rewarding goals and strengthens the positive feelings rewards can provide. Dopamine makes us desire things that we believe will benefit us—and reward us with a surge of feel-good natural chemicals when we get those things. When we are hungry, dopamine strongly suggests we eat. Thirsty? Drink.

Dopamine is responsible for our desire for sex, food, and winning competitions. And to add fuel to the fire, THC, the major psychoactive component in cannabis, increases the release of dopamine, which lowers inhibitions and enhances the feeling of pleasure; giving us more, better. Dr. Lieberman shares in his recent book, "Most people when they think of dopamine, they think about pleasure, but it's so much more. Dopamine can do wonderful things—it gives us energy, motivation, desire, excitement, confidence. It can also do terrible things. It makes us dissatisfied, unhappy, miserable, and constantly chasing something we can never capture."[88] In *The Molecule of More*, Dr. Lieberman talks about dopamine as a molecule of more and examines situations in which the brain asks for more of something after the novelty of what you just received has worn off.

Dopamine makes our brain believe that, in getting a thing, our life will somehow be better than it is right now. Sometimes the thrill of what's next is so enticing, it literally cannot be ignored. This is the essence of compulsivity. What lasting impact will you allow these psychological influences to have on your financial future?

Reason 28

The Personal Entourage:
Everybody's Invited to the Party

Kings, queens, dukes, duchesses, the Pope, and the president of the United States have their own entourages to cater to their every need. Even Jesus had an entourage—his 12 disciples—primarily to mentor and educate. Fast-forward to 1993: Benny "The Jet" Rodriguez arrived on the scene with his entourage in the box office hit *Sandlot*, and we loved it. Humans are relational beings, and most of us enjoy communing in familiar groups and living in active social circles, or tribes. It's likely your tribe started to form during adolescence and continued to solidify during young adulthood, representing your inaugural entourage. There are two primary entourage categories: the personal crew and the professional crew.

Earlier, I discussed the importance of being surrounded by people who love you and respect you, and a crew of competent professionals who want to see you succeed. Your current personal entourage has access to you; they feed your mind and influence your behavior on the regular. Social proximity suggests your friends' habits will become your habits. Hence, to build good habits, spend more time with people who already practice good habits. Do you have friends who have the capacity to sabotage your future?

People want to hang out with professional athletes as a member of their entourage for a myriad of reasons. Athletes are fun to be around. They have life experiences many do not have, they tell great stories, they are usually very charismatic, they have great physical presence, and they live aspirational lifestyles. From what former entourage members have shared with me, the top two reasons pro athletes attract members into their inner circle are (1) they are magnets for beautiful ladies and

(2) they usually foot the hefty drinking tabs at the clubs. The established entourage includes the encourager, the mentor, the accountability partner, the trainer, the moral compass, the best friend, the challenger, FAM, the wingman, homeboys/homies, the bodyguard/the problem-solver, former high school and collegiate teammates, partners, and, yes, random hangers-on and maybe even hood rats. This may not be an exhaustive list.

On a similar note, professional athletes want to be surrounded by people who like them because they are people, too. It's human nature to want to be connected to others. Elite athletes, even the most accomplished ones, want to be included and feel like a member of the tribe. It just feels better than isolation; no one wants to feel left out. Everyone wants to be loved, accepted, appreciated, relevant, heard, and seen, and to feel safe. During the first few years in the pros, you may need a confidant, someone to confide in and keep your secrets, someone to hang, travel, and eat with, and who genuinely cares about you. In this light, the personal entourage serves a very important social role in your life: to help you stay connected.

When is the entourage potentially bad? *When everybody's invited.* Problems arise when the support system becomes toxic—when some members of your entourage no longer serve your interests and then start to take advantage of the relationship. You may experience a drain of your financial resources when you're followed by too many individuals and are expected to financially support people who are hanging around for the ride and the free stuff. Be vigilant of posse members who are always expecting free dinners, constantly asking for financial favors, requesting loans without supplying collateral, insisting you invest in unvetted business schemes, or asking you to facilitate nefarious arrangements that may damage your reputation and deplete your finances.

Better Ways to Deal with a Personal Entourage

- Limit the number in your inner circle.
- Select only a few to go out for dinner or drinks.
- Only take out the larger crew on limited or special occasions.

- Assign someone the "people counter" (to count the number in your party before you sit down), to discourage others from joining the group because the drinks are free.
- Have someone strong in math to be the bill checker to check to make sure the final bill is accurate and to ensure extra items were not added to *your* restaurant/bar tab.
- Encourage your entourage party to not invite people (like ex-girlfriends, neighbors, or barbers) to join the group (to impress them) without your knowledge.
- Hire responsible members of the entourage and turn them into employees. Then establish rules of engagement, behavior expectations, and work assignments to make them accountable. (You benefit by having solid employees and meaningful tax deductions.)
- Encourage members to start a business and use their services as independent contractors.
- Choose members of your circle wisely.

> *"Do not be misled: bad company corrupts good character."*
>
> —1 Corinthians 15:33 (NIV)

Words to the wise:
There are relationships you outgrow over time. It may be necessary for your personal and financial well-being to expedite the pruning process.

Reason 29

Big Tip Energy

When you enter a business, car dealership, or retail store, they notice you right away. It's impossible to hide from smartphone cameras and prying eyes when you are a famous, elite athlete. Because of social profiling, you look different than other consumers; you have an appearance of success and money. When out for a nice, quiet dinner with your family, be on the lookout for charming but opportunistic maître d's and assistant general managers who want to be of service *any way they can*. Even the waitstaff may start to salivate thinking about a possible big tip. If you are not mindful of the big tip energy at your favorite eating place, you can be in for an expensive game of chicken. Cha-ching.

Everyone has a restaurant tip story. Here's mine:

It was a beautiful early evening downtown Chicago in October 2013, and our family was celebrating. Brandon, recently graduated from the University of Illinois, went undrafted in the 2013 NBA draft but, having had success in the NBA Summer League, was delighted to compare offers he received from NBA general managers with what he could get playing overseas in the vast international basketball ecosystem.

According to his agent, Brandon hit the international basketball jackpot, and he signed a fully guaranteed contract to play for a team in Nizhny Novgorod, Russia. They offered Brandon the highest contract of any first-year player playing overseas in 2013. We were so elated. (Aside: Many international teams pay the income taxes for their U.S. players, thereby allowing American basketball players to enjoy tax-free

157

income from their teams abroad. Additionally, many top international teams provide free lodging and a new car for their signees. Sweet deal.)

I planned a three-day sendoff—a family celebration downtown Chicago for Brandon as he was starting his professional basketball career in a land far, far away. We took the train to Chicago (I love the Metra) and stayed at the JW Marriott Chicago (my favorite hotel in Chicago). Our plans included a shopping trip on the Magnificent Mile, attending the musical *Book of Mormon,* and of course our celebratory dinner at a nice steakhouse in the theater district. We chose Rosebud Prime on Dearborn. Hubby Cliff and I had had a great experience there months before as Brandon was going through the 2013 NBA Draft Combine in Chicago and were treated very well by Brandon's former agent, Jim Tanner, and the restaurant's waitstaff.

On our return visit, I had a little different experience. The food was very good and the waitstaff presentation was on point. A few of the guests and employees recognized Brandon, and there was some chatter as we were seated. I fully planned to pay for the meal, but I had the brilliant idea to use the meal as a teachable moment for Brandon. I asked him to pay the bill and I would reimburse him after dinner. I wanted to teach Brandon how to look at the bill—not just glance at the final amount, but actually study it to make sure it appeared accurate, without taking out a calculator. Okay, so I wish I had taken out the calculator. I had invited family friends/new client, the Caples, to dinner with us. After dinner and during my sendoff conversation with the Caples, I looked over to see Brandon paying the bill. I got caught up in entertaining my guests and I did not view the bill to demonstrate how to study the final check. I failed in my teachable moment. Consequently, Brandon paid a handsome tip *on top of* the 18% gratuity that was already assessed to the final check for our small party of eight.

After dinner, when I asked to see the check, Brandon only had the card copy with the final amount. Apparently the waitstaff kept the detailed dinner tab. Urggg. The final amount was higher than what I expected, and seeing that I had promised to reimburse him, I was not happy that the waitstaff did not tell us the restaurant's new policy that an 18% gratuity is added on parties of eight (prior, it was for parties of 12 or more), nor did they make any effort to confirm with Brandon if he was aware of the restaurant's new gratuity policy after seeing the generous tip. In my disappointment and disbelief, when I returned to my hotel room, I immediately called the restaurant to see if I could get a copy of the full bill. Yeah, I was feeling my feelings at this time. Because they were "busy," the person on the other end of the phone suggested I call the next morning to talk with the general manager. The GM strung me along a few days before finally apologizing for the system's inability to reproduce the full bill.

Much to my chagrin, I had to give up my hunt for the truth. Was it an error or an expectation? The food and (non-alcoholic) beverage bill was just under $800, and gratuities were paid on that amount. While I chalked this experience up to "my bad," the lesson I learned was a costly one, as I reimbursed Brandon as promised. This experience has stuck in my craw to this day. The good news is, if you ever see Brandon out at dinner or clubbing, you best be assured he will study the final bill for accuracy, pull out his calculator, look to see if a gratuity or service charge was already applied, and *then* tip appropriately. A teachable moment indeed.

Up for debate: As a well-paid pro athlete, do you think you should be expected to pay more in tips because you can afford to pay more? Do you tip the same percentage regardless of the level of service you receive? Do you feel a twinge of guilt or shame, therefore adding a much higher tip, because you don't want to be thought of as cheap? Do you usually pay more than a 20% tip on bar tabs with no food? Should you? It's a classic case of big tip energy and big tip expectations: Everybody wants a piece of you and your wallet. If tips are discretionary and voluntary, what is the proper tip etiquette for highly compensated jocks?

What about the other millionaires, the nameless highly paid software engineers, doctors, attorneys, entrepreneurs, general managers, and C-suite members who dine at restaurants and consume other services but are not known by the public because they generally are not 6'9"? Should they also be *expected* to tip according to their ability to pay? Is it fair that pro athletes are generally expected to "give back" in excess every time they have an encounter with the working class?

Words to the wise:

Find a balance when you are dealing with restaurants and others in the service industry like baristas, personal shoppers, cab/Uber/Lyft drivers, valet workers, doormen/doorwomen, hostesses, security guards at clubs, barbers, and masseuses. Look to make sure your final bill is accurate and tip according to the level of service you receive. Don't be socially bullied to give more.

It is hard to find size 16 bowling shoes

Family dinner

Reason 30

Turnt Up with Fam: VIP Bottle Service

I Got You

You want to be liked and admired. You want to share your career and financial success with your fam and friends, and show how happy you are and how much you've appreciated their support over the years. When celebrating, a night on the town should be a special occasion, the full monty, but this extravagance should not be an everyday occurrence. Enjoy life on your terms but do so in moderation and in a responsible manner. Before going out, decide how much you plan to spend and stick with your plan. If you do not plan in advance, you are likely to spend more than you expected and be disappointed with yourself for overspending.

> *The following is recounted from son #1, Cliff Jr., about a night in the life of a pro athlete and his homies.*

A Night to Remember

It's Halloween 2018. My frat brother, a business associate, and myself were all chillin' at a friend's party. The party was packed; a few of my college friends were there; it was fun and things were rockin'. Two hours in, Brandon texted me and said he had a table at Tao, a premiere nightclub downtown Chicago. The club was only a few miles from where we were. I had to pull up. I told him I had two other people with me and he said, "Any girls?" I said yes, plus my ship (line brother). He said, "I got y'all. Text me when you're outside."

We swung over there in a Lyft ride, and when we arrived outside around midnight it was pandemonium. It was dark. There were at least 200 people outside the entrance of the club trying to get in. I fought my way to the security side of the entrance, but that area was also packed with people begging the security crew to get in. I told Brandon we were outside, and he said, "Daniel is coming down for you. Look for him."

Filled with excitement and anticipation, I waited for my security escort to Brandon's table inside the club. I was looking over at the crowd of people still trying to talk themselves into the club. The scene was unreal. Then I saw Chance the Rapper, his wife (girlfriend at the time), and 10 of their friends pull up. Man, they were right beside me. Huge fan—didn't want to be thirsty—but I was excited. Daniel then emerged from the club with about 20 additional members of the security staff—literally 15 bouncers and five security personnel grabbing VIPs from the crowd outside the side entrance. Daniel motioned us over. I was like, "Dude, Chance is here." Daniel was like, "Ha ha, he has to wait a little." He walked me through Tao with my friends—a huge club packed head to toe with people. Many of the people were in decked out Halloween costumes.

[After] what seemed like a half-mile walk around the side walls and through people, we got to the VIP tables by the DJ, where I saw BP. He greeted me warmly. I recognized a few people at his table like his trainer and a few other friends, then all I saw was girls, girls, girls. I said what's up. I introduced my friends, and everyone immediately demanded we pour ourselves drinks from the literal endless supply of refreshing beverages. I turned to see the waitstaff bring more bottles with sparklers, announcing their arrival. I heard glasses clinking, beverages being poured, and the DJ throwing down the hits.

Crazy nightclubbing ensued. Next thing I knew, two Chicago Bulls players came around Brandon's table. Then the table next to us, which appeared to be the last open table, got filled by Chance The Rapper and his crew. Everyone was having a blast. The DJ was on fire. I was 10 feet from Chance and between us was his security. With my reach and positioning I could've easily tapped Chance to ask for a selfie.

Instead, a drunk, *self-conscious* me asked his security for permission and he said no. Damn. The party continued without me getting a selfie, the drinks kept coming, and the DJ kept things popping. Fun fun fun all night. Got our Lyft around 3:30 a.m. and it's a wrap! I will always remember that Halloween night at Tao's bottle service VIP section. It was a blast. Best nightclub experience ever. EVER.

_____

Bottle service is a special experience for nightclub/bar guests that allows them to purchase drinks by the bottle. Bottle service is all the rage in the nightlife of the pro athlete. In exchange for buying bottles instead of drinks by the glass, the paying customer receives reserved seating, a bottle server (or two), security, and a variety of drink mixers. While the arrangement is called bottle service, the real attraction is the reserved seating and the appearance of VIP status. Often, the reserved seating has luxurious upholstery, private cabanas, and ropes/stanchions to separate VIP bottle service guests from the rest of the partygoers. It also gives the bottle service guests a feel of exclusivity. According to WebstaurantStore.com, some clubs even place the bottle service area on a raised platform, giving the guests a great vantage point for checking out the action all throughout the club.

Of course, all this exclusivity comes with a price. The price of bottles is generally marked up 20 times the cost—but guests with financial means are happy to pay this premium for these party perks. Let's do the math: a night out with friends, beautiful ladies, and a 15-person entourage, can end with a $3,000–25,000 tab. What do you tip on a $25,000 bottle service bar tab? Also, who is keeping track of the number of bottles being delivered to the table? How do you know the final bill is accurate? My guess is, after the third drink, no one really cares. And the party goes on, and on, and on…

The harder it is to get into a popular club, the higher the cost for the bottle service. The higher the cost for the bottle service, the more attractive it is for professional athletes. If a club can attract a good number of pro athletes, the more popular the club becomes—and the bottle service competition is on. It's a delicious economic master class in supply and demand.

Words to the wise:
Enjoy yourself and your fam, in moderation. The more money you spend on bottle service, the less money you will have to take advantage of the power of compounding interest/the Rule of 72. See Reason #26.

Cliff Jr. and Brandon with Chef Nusret aka Salt Bae

Reason 31

Bruh, You Extra

From Dorm Room to 10,000-Square-Foot Mansion

You've heard the phrase *Money can't buy happiness*. Turns out this may not be entirely true. Money can buy things that can bring about a certain degree of life satisfaction, thereby creating a sense of happiness. Studies indicate emotional well-being rises with income, and spending money on experiences and things that align with our values can increase the potential for happiness. Shopping is considered a great stress reliever by many—hence the term *retail therapy*. We feel happier when we shop. Many businesses embrace consumerism by promoting all-day shopping themes like Black Friday, Cyber Monday, Amazon Prime Day, Small Business Saturday, and Singles Day (Alibaba), to encourage spending behavior and boost economic activity. Who doesn't love shopping and spending money? According to clinical psychologist Scott Bea, PsyD, "research suggests there's actually a lot of psychological and therapeutic value when you're shopping—if done in moderation, of course."[89]

According to Dr. Bea, cited in the health archives of the Cleveland Clinic,[90] we get a psychological and emotional boost when we shop. This is because:

1. Shopping restores a sense of control over our environment.
2. Shopping eases feelings of sadness.
3. Shopping stimulates the senses—all of them! Visualization/the smell of something new distracts us from anxiety and gets us to visualize positive outcomes.
4. Dopamine is released from the brain even before a purchase is made—so planning a purchase is equally pleasurable.

5. No surprise, online shopping gives the most satisfaction, as we get a dopamine hit planning the purchase, another one when we actually buy it, and then another rush waiting for our package to arrive (the anticipation). We experience dopamine-fueled excitement at each moment of the shopping experience.[91]

As with all pleasurable activities, like eating sugary treats, having sex, exercising, and shopping, where the rewards are felt throughout our entire body thanks to dopamine, too much could be detrimental to the mind, body, and wallet.

Compulsive Spending

When we think about something compulsive, we think about obsessive or irresistible urges, or perhaps we think of people who are addicted or otherwise dependent on mind-altering drugs, alcohol, shopping, gambling, and sex. How can spending or otherwise-fun experiences turn into addictive traps? The act of buying for yourself and others triggers a release of dopamine. Dopamine is a part of our reward system, and when released in the body plays a role in how we feel pleasure.

People who constantly and excessively pursue what they believe to be the things that will give them the most pleasure may have a certain personality trait. According to studies cited in the book *Molecule of More,* there may be some evidence that this may be true. According to the research discussed in the book, people who have the D4 gene, 7R variant tend to be people who are novelty seeking, are less tolerant of monotony, and pursue whatever is new and unusual. They can be impulsive, exploratory, fickle, excitable, quick-tempered, and extravagant.[92] Sound like someone you know?

By spending hard-earned money on things you desire, you give yourself an opportunity to mentally escape from the stresses of everyday life. In response to your purchasing behavior, you are rewarded with immediate pleasure and satisfaction, more perceived happiness, and dopamine-fueled excitement felt throughout the body. Some young, elite athletes have a strong but unrealistic feeling that the money from their sport career will keep coming in, and therefore they spend more. And with every dollar of spending, that feel-good energy races throughout their bodies, urging more and more spending behavior just like before; lather, rinse, and repeat. Insatiable.

Too much of a good thing can be too much. Excessive shopping shifts from pleasurable to problematic when it is combined with compulsive behaviors, OCD (obsessive compulsive disorder), or the mindset that enough can never be enough. Expensive cars, expansive homes, an extravagant wardrobe of designer clothes, flashy jewelry, and consuming high-priced convenience for convenience's sake can be a recipe for financial disaster. If purchasing behaviors are not managed properly, spending can get out of control and lead to you living a life beyond your means—and into the financial abyss.

Words to the wise:
Informal surveys claim the number-one reason that pro athletes go broke is they spend beyond their means. Here's how to fix this: Adopt *a now and later* spending habit. Spend a lot less than you earn **now,** living below your means, so your frontloaded earnings can stretch far into the future, for *later* consumption. Make it a priority to buy (invest in) appreciating assets and spend less on depreciating and disposable goods.
Next time you go shopping, ask yourself: Will this expensive thing I want to purchase increase in value over time? If the answer is no, **pause** and reevaluate if you should follow through with that purchase. Remember the goal is to *be* rich, not necessarily *look* rich.

CHAPTER 5

Physical and Mental Health

Forever Young?

Health is wealth. Can't have one without the other. You're in the public eye; people expect you to be great—exceptional. You push your body to the limits to stay competitive. It's all about the wins—the outcomes. You are strong, fearless, tenacious. You've been groomed to be laser-focused on your journey to greatness. You live a healthy and productive life. You are learning how to sustain success throughout your career. You have already made a commitment to train and exercise regularly, attend yoga and stretching sessions, eat a healthy diet of clean foods, avoid or reduce sugar intake, and drink lots of water. You are doing all the things that you believe will keep you healthy. Kudos. Russell Wilson, NFL quarterback of the Denver Bronco, says he spends $1 million dollars a year to train his body and, at age 33, admits the primary reason for this investment in his physical conditioning is he hopes to play in the NFL until he's 45 years old.[93] The importance of training and staying vigilant about your physical well-being are discussed ad nauseam during your personal and team conditioning sessions. It's understood by elite athletes around the globe that good health brings more opportunities to monetize your sport's career – to keep the financial resources flowing.

Steadfastness and stamina are revered as keys to victory. But physical prowess is only one aspect of overall wellness. An equally important part of health and well-being that oftentimes gets overlooked or ignored is mental health. Elite athletes are coming to grips with the idea that working on the mind is just as important as working out the body. "Mind over matter" can bring a competitive edge in sports and in your financial decision-making. It's good to know that being on top of your physical and mental game will give you the stamina needed to constantly improve your professional brand and expand your financial positioning, leading to a long sports career and a prosperous future.

> *"It's a process. It's a lifestyle. I think that when you're trying to play as long as I'm trying to play— for me, the mentality, the focus level, everything that you have to do has to be surrounded on that. The biggest thing for me is the mental game. You know, the mental game is so important."*[94]
>
> —Russell Wilson, NFL quarterback of the Denver Broncos

What about *your* mental game? Every action you take is observed carefully by your coaching staff, the media, and sport fans around the world, resulting in a life that resembles being in a fishbowl. The pressure to be, act, and do "right" can be so unnerving, it can lead a young elite athlete to make decisions that may not be in his best interest, in an attempt to escape or run for cover. Pervasive mental challenges suffered by pro athletes include excessive stress, eating disorders, anxiety, burnout, attention-seeking, insecurities, depression, loneliness, low self-esteem, and low self-worth. Many are living on the very edge of familiarity; one push can take them over that edge into uncharted waters. The disappointment of not measuring up to others' expectations can thrust the young athlete into compulsive behaviors like excessive spending, gambling, reckless alcohol, and drug use.

In the water, Olympic swimming champion Michael Phelps was spectacular, earning 23 gold medals from 2001 to 2019, but out of his gifted element, he experienced difficult challenges. In 2014, he was arrested for a second DUI in 10 years. He says, "I was a train wreck, man. I was just like a time bomb waiting to go off. Man, I had no self-esteem, no self-worth. For a moment, I thought it was going to be the end of my life. Literally. I figured the best thing to do is to end my life."[95]

Photo Credit: Michael Dalder / Reuters

Michael Phelps, Olympic Gold Medal Winner

Buzz Aldrin, American astronaut with NASA (*Apollo 11*), with Neil Armstrong, was one of the first two people to land on the moon. After retiring from space travel, Buzz became the National Association for Mental Health (NAMH) chairman and spoke around the country about his mental health challenges. He described how his life started to fall apart without having the constant challenges of working for the space industry and successfully solving important problems. "When you're used to having most things go right, it's difficult suddenly to face anything going wrong. Depression, something I thought only happened to other people, was happening to me."[96]

> *"I thought I made some tough decisions in my life, but now, I was facing something which was probably my biggest [decision]. The decision to seek professional help for my emotional problems."*[97]
>
> —Buzz Aldin, American astronaut

This may be a parallel case for young pro athletes: As you live out your formative sporting years, sheltered by trusted adults / handlers, everything appears to work out for you, no matter the circumstance. Then you reach the professional ranks and things are not what you expected. The pressure, among other things, can be paralyzing. Mental health issues are real, common, *and* treatable. Own your stuff, then get help. This chapter identifies mental issues that can trip you up and cause you to make unwise decisions, negatively impacting your sport career / personal and professional brand. Self-care is important for your physical and mental well-being, ultimately leading to a much-improved financial well-being.

Mastering your emotional and physical health is the currency you need to live your best life imaginable. Without adequate attention paid to these things, you risk suffering burnout, leading to poor performance, a shortened professional sports career, and possible missed lucrative opportunities, which can leave you financially ill-prepared for the future.

Invest in yourself: your physical body, your mental health, and your fiscal health, including making the commitment to learn about money even beyond reading this book. Manage the mind games, so you don't sabotage your professional career and your financial future. Be disciplined in your approach to keeping your mind and body game ready. Remember: If you stay ready, you don't have to get ready.

> *"By far the best investment you can make is in yourself."*
>
> —Warren Buffett

Reason 32

Ego

"Mean" Joe Greene. The Grim Reaper. Night
Train. "Hitman" Hearns. The Dominator. The
Assassin. The Intimidator. Boom-Boom.
Beast Mode. Ironhead. Nigerian Nightmare.
The Greatest. Black Mamba. King James.

Sport nicknames speak volumes of the toughness one needs to compete at the highest level. The expression *Attitude is everything* does not go far enough to speak to what it takes for an elite athlete to take center stage among his peers. It requires talent, passion, perseverance, and years of training to get to the top of your game. Once you've arrived, it's mentally grueling to keep up with the pressure that comes along with being the best of the best. So what is the "X factor" for epic success? Psychologist Angela Lee Duckworth speaks of *grit* being one of the dominant personality traits that can determine whether you succeed at your goals.[98] Self-confidence is also believed to be a must-have mental attribute to reach a higher level. There is great benefit being confident in your abilities and your skills when dealing with a competitive environment, but can you become overconfident?

Ego—the identity that your mind creates about yourself; a strong and healthy sense of self. Many psychologists call the ego the decision-making component of our personality. It's the thing that makes you,

you. Ego can be a good thing or bad thing. When it's good, it fuels confidence and can be that "X factor" enabling you to compete at the highest level. But what if that ego becomes unmanageable and turns into overconfidence? An outsized belief in our own importance can make our ego take concern about ourselves, an important aspect of self-perseverance, and turn it into an obsession—all about me, me, me. Pat Riley, an NBA Hall of Fame coach, coined the unhealthy ego as the *disease of me*. Our ego asserts itself when we pursue great things or when we achieve noteworthy success, like becoming a lottery pick in the NBA draft, winning the World Cup, being named the Super Bowl MVP, or dominating Wimbledon.

In the world of the ego, outcomes are very important. It may not let you rest on your laurels, as it always wants more. After achieving exceptional prominence in the sport world, the ego can make one believe that there will always be continuing success, which can lead to overconfidence. Many sport experts believe that the line between confidence and overconfidence/arrogance is as fine as the line between success and failure in high level competition. In your unique situation, in which compensation is primarily performance-based (including salaries, signing bonuses, incentives, and endorsements), a strong, healthy ego can benefit you greatly and can improve your leadership opportunities and negotiation prowess.

The ego is tricky. If left unchecked, the ego can take an eruption of confidence and turn it into arrogance, leading to cockiness and boastful, flamboyant, and risky behaviors. A bloated ego can sabotage personal aspirations and long-term goals, damage your personal and professional brand, blow lucrative business opportunities, and limit gains in your personal finances.

Words to the wise:
Keep your ego in check by ascribing to The Shamrock System—Plus Minus, and Equal offered by legendary MMA fighter Frank Shamrock:[99]   1. <u>Plus</u>: Learn from someone with more experience than you—to remember that there is always someone better than you are. This will instill humility.   2. <u>Minus</u>: Teach someone with less experience than you. This will help you look objectively at your failures and compile lessons to pass on to others who aspire to do great things.   3. <u>Equal</u>: Engage and connect with someone with the same experience as you. This will encourage you to seek better competitive opportunities and to take more time looking for ways to improve your game, and less time obsessing over public opinion on social media.

Reason 33

FOMO (Fear of Missing Out)

It's a week after you signed your contract. You wake up and you have feelings of elation. You've achieved a level you've dreamed of most of your life. You're getting congratulatory calls, text messages, and IG shout-outs, but all you can think is "Why am I not as happy as I should be? Am I missing something?" You see other pro athletes enjoying their newly acquired wealth—all on full display on social media. As you click away, you see your friends at parties, an ex-girlfriend modeling new shoes, a teammate showing off his new sports car, and even the team owner enjoying a ride on his candy apple red yacht. From your POV, *everyone* is living the life. Your current situation is sitting on a boring couch, reading your humdrum playbook, and preparing for your tedious training and conditioning sessions, long-drawn-out team meetings, and other mundane activities drummed up by your agent. Is this it?

If you've ever felt like there must be more, you might have been experiencing FOMO. The fear of missing out refers to the feeling or perception that others are having more fun and living better lives than you are. FOMO may bring about a feeling of anxiety when we see something exciting and aspirational happing in our social and professional circles, and we are not a part of it. Social media gives us instant access to our friends, family, neighbors, coworkers, and love interests. This can be a good thing, but, if we are not careful, we might start to compare our everyday lives to what our friends post on social media platforms, which is most likely the best of their cleverly curated life's highlight reel. Ever notice no one posts their daily routines or uninteresting activities? This oranges-to-apples comparison can bring on a sense of insecurity and a feeling that you are missing out on the good stuff. In a zealous reaction, you might get the urge to get more connected by accepting invitations to parties you don't want to attend, going on trips you don't want to go on, hanging out with people you do not like, and doing stuff that is not your thing. FOMO is a real phenomenon.

The fear component in FOMO can cause you to make bad decisions, keep your schedule unnecessarily full, cause you to spend money on stuff that does not bring you pleasure, flood your mind with stress, and can even lead to depression. There is so much going on. Our imaginations are constantly bombarding our minds with scenarios that appear better than our current reality. Are you getting stock and business investment tips, urging you to act now? Tempted to show up to appear (unpaid) at product launches? Feeling a need to check out that dope late-night party you saw on your IG feed—the night before a big game or match? Getting "discounted" offers on that smokin' Ferrari Roma Blu in your DMs? Someone wants you to check out that dope beach house in Miami? Even your wingman got someone for you to meet…twins! Having concerns you might miss out on the next big thing or afraid you'll miss an opportunity of a lifetime can lead to making irrational choices and you can easily be manipulated by others.

Slow your roll. Resist the feeling that your life is not exciting. Don't allow your happiness and life satisfaction to be falsely diminished. Take caution not to make poor decisions about spending your time and money based on a flawed mindset. Find ways to quiet the dopaminergic hype and protect yourself from time killers by creating your own schedule to include things you genuinely like to do, places you want to go, interesting people you want to hang around and learn from, and events that promote your personal and professional brands. Learn how to say no to things that do not serve you, take regular breaks from social media, change your focus from what you lack to what you have, and practice gratitude. Don't get enticed to buy something, sign something, or invest in something because you are scared if you don't, you'll be missing out. More isn't always better. There will be another opportunity.

Words to the wise:
A lot of people want to be like the "cool kids"; they want to go where they go and do the things they do. Guess what? You're already among the coolest on the planet. Download the Audible app and listen to an interesting book or find a worthwhile hobby to expand your mind. With an ever-expanding brain, there's really no room for *FOMO* intrusive thoughts.

Reason 34

Imposter Syndrome

> *"Uh oh, they're going to find out now. I've run a game on everybody, and they're going to find me out."*
>
> —Maya Angelou, famed poet and Civil Rights activist, admitting her struggles with imposter syndrome

Ever wonder why you were the only one out of many gifted elite athletes to sign a lucrative professional contract? Why you? Was it skill? Luck? Did someone make a mistake?

Do you experience self-doubt or engage in negative self-talk? Do you sometimes think you are undeserving / unworthy of your achievements and the accolades that you receive from your peers, the coaching staff, and the fans? Do you have a persistent feeling that sneaks into your conscious mind that you are not really as good as others think you are? Do you have trouble accepting praise or hide awards, shun or discount accomplishments? If any of these situations haunt you, you may be experiencing imposter syndrome. Imposter syndrome is a psychological mindset that brings an onslaught of chronic self-doubt, thoughts of insecurity, questioning of skills, a feeling of incompetence, inadequacy, and uncertainty about your talents and abilities. These feelings scream self-destructive thoughts that *you don't belong—that you are a fraud.*

Everyone has fears and doubts. As success grows and the prize gets closer, fear starts to rear its unrelenting head – bullying the otherwise successful achiever to have second thoughts about his own ability to level up. To move pass self-sabotage to attain greater heights, it's imperative that the young elite athlete stay laser-focused and believe his beliefs and doubt his doubts. But with the imposter phenomenon, thoughts can get twisted, he may instead start to believe his doubts and doubt his beliefs.

These unwanted internal thoughts and silent actions brought on by this imposter mindset can lead to the belief that you've fooled others into believing you are someone you aren't—that you are a fraud. This brand of cognitive dissonance is uncomfortable and result in a feeling of unease, leading you to engage in inappropriate behavior to cope and escape low self-worth, and act out in ways that could harm your reputation and professional brand. This can derail your dreams and aspirations and shortchange your financial potential.

We often measure our own well-being based on how we see others doing. If others appear to be doing better than we are, we automatically diminish our accomplishments. Even with outstanding personal accomplishments, imposter syndrome leaves the pro athlete with a sense of being inauthentically accomplished — making him minimize the success he worked so hard to achieve, leading to a thought that he is undeserving of accolades and will fail to live up to the expectation of other people.

We all have an inner critic. According to the National Science Foundation the average person has about 12,000 to 60,000 thoughts per day. Of those, 80% are negative and 95% are exactly the same repetitive thoughts as the day before.[100] Trouble comes when these feelings of self-doubt are chronic. Exhale. Don't internalize negative thoughts. If this chronic self-doubt is not put in check, the constant negativity can diminish self-worth and choke confidence. Negative thoughts impact your performance, decision-making, relationships, health, level of happiness, and long-term success.[101] Other consequences of this mindset are mood swings, anxiety, and an increased level of stress. People overcompensate chronic self-doubt by over-training, becoming a perfectionist, and over-committing. This can lead to exhaustion, job burnout, and depression. Financially speaking, these consequences can lead to poor performance, a diminished professional brand, and reduced leverage during contract negotiation.

Can imposter syndrome be a form of perfectionism, a focus on being flawless and a strong desire to impress? Overachievers mostly always experience fear and self-doubt in the face of attaining higher goals. Having certain emotional reactions after winning a championship, breaking an athletic record, or achieving some lofty career goal does not sound like a syndrome at all, but a natural reaction to life's challenges when you are leveling up. Nothing is wrong with you; you are simply having a human experience. We win and lose, we rise and fall, we laugh and cry, we have adversities and triumphs—all are a part of our expansion and growth. Catherine Harmon Toomer, MD defends the mindset: "When a person excels time and time again in the face of fear, self-doubt or when feeling like a fraud, it is the epitome of strength, courage and bravery."[102]

Words to the wise:

You are worthy of success. Accomplishments don't create your worthiness, they reveal it. God ordained your worth when you were born; it's indisputable. We start life worthy to be here and to achieve at the highest level, and we stay worthy throughout our lives. Own it.

Photo Credit: Spurs official release

League MVP vs. Rookie, don't doubt

Reason 35

YOLO: Mavericks and Excessive Gambling

Technical Foul: Unsportsmanlike Conduct

In 1980, Rosie Ruiz placed first in the 84th Boston Marathon. It was a hug win for Ruiz until it came out that she had cheated and jumped into the race from somewhere in the crowd along the marathon route, close to the finish line. Did she think people in the crowd wouldn't notice someone jumping into the race, especially if that someone went on to win? The course-cutter was ultimately stripped of her victory and went on to become known in running circles as "the cheater."

Wildin', living on the edge, risk-taking, casting caution to the wind, living dangerously, flirting with danger, playing Russian roulette, thrill-seeking, winning at all costs, trendsetting, being cutting edge—a maverick's contemporary modus operandi. Mavericks are those individuals who are unconventional and independent, they do not think or behave in the same way as other people, and do not go along with the group. They sometimes display rebellious, reckless and disruptive behaviors with fanatical agendas. Sometimes pro athletes behave like mavericks, sprinting to the cliff with reckless abandon; engaging in irresponsible behaviors, dumb stunts, and foolish actions; and spewing unfiltered words for shock value. In contrast, some mavericks are bold visionaries and want to achieve great things. The line between bold and reckless is razor thin. It takes nastiness, cockiness, and mettle to earn the reputation of a bad boy in sports. These are interestingly the same qualities needed to be a great competitor at the highest level.

If you ask a pro athlete why he likes living on the edge, he might answer that he loves the challenge of getting out of his comfort zone, and it's his unique way of making moves toward greatness. Or he might also say he does not want to limit himself based on self-imposed or society-imposed limitations. Some elite athletes suffer from young person's disease—invincibility. They often try to push the boundaries, with little regard to consequences. To try to understand why, we need to look at how our brain is wired. The brain is composed of three main sections that function at three different levels: our lower brain, which controls our most basic unconscious and automatic functions for physical survival (breathing, movement, heartbeat, and blood flow); our mid-level brain, which creates and controls emotions, stores short- and long-term memories, and is responsible for motivation and our survival instincts; and our high-level brain, which is the logic center that is responsible for reasoning, problem-solving, planning, creativeness, and high-level communication. These three sections are very distinct and do very different things, but they have a synergistic relationship.

When it comes to making decisions that brings immediate pleasure, our brain operates in what is coined the motivational triad. Basically, the brain is motivated by three deeply rooted survival instincts: to seek pleasure, to avoid pain, and to complete activities as efficiently as possible (as not to expend too much energy). This motivation to seek pleasure trumps the higher-level brain intellectual engagements and gives our lower brain the advantage when faced with decisions that involves immediate pleasure. It's physiology.

It's happening right in front of your eyes, every day. Well-compensated elite athletes are making bad decisions that have financial and reputational consequences and yet their athletic production on the field / court / ice is applauded. These decisions include irresponsible behaviors, unproductive and dumb habits, foolish actions, and being naively outspoken on politically sensitive topics. *Irresponsible behaviors* (e.g., having unprotected sex, participating in a team headbutting celebration after a touchdown), *dumb habits* (e.g., getting drunk in public and getting arrested for driving under the influence, betting against your own team, buying drugs in public, cheating by not putting in real effort), *foolish actions* (e.g., insulting the team's chefs, having pictures taken while you are doing drugs, shooting yourself in the leg while showing off your gun, slamming your pitching thumb with a hammer, headbutting an opponent two days before your contract signing date, leaving your playbook in your "girlfriend's" apartment, taking steroids and lying about it under oath), and using ill-advised *unfiltered words* (e.g., insulting fans via social media, sharing TMI, getting into a "dozens" brawl with an ESPN talking head, predicting a team loss on twitter, boasting about your intelligence) may all have consequences.

We are inundated with stories of bad boys in sports. The narrative tragically goes like this: professional athletes behaving badly, then their subsequent fall from fame. The competitive nature of sports seems to bring out the worst in some athletes who appear to feed on anger and aggression to raise their level of play. Trouble arises when this anger, aggression, and one-upmanship spirals out of control.

NFL quarterback Michael Vick, also known for dog fighting and illegal betting, served 21 months in federal prison. Antonio Cassano, an international soccer player, known for his womanizing, short-tempered outbursts, and disputes / confrontation with managers and teammates, lost it all. One of the best-known bad boys of professional sports is cyclist Lance Armstrong. Blood doping, cheating, bribing officials, and a "win at all costs" mentality in pursuit of fame cost him everything. Armstrong "won" the Tour de France seven consecutive times from 1999 to 2005 but was later stripped of all titles when an investigation revealed he used—to which he later admitted—performance-enhancing drugs. In 2012, Armstrong was handed a lifetime ban from the sport he loved.

When Armstrong was asked why he and many of his U.S. cohorts decided to use banned substances, the Texan said it was his belief that they needed to dope up to compete in Europe: "We did what we had to do to win." Armstrong continues, "I knew there were going to be knives, and then one day, people start showing up with guns. That's when you say, 'Do [you] either fly back to Plano, Texas, and not know what you're going to do? Or do you walk over to the gun store?' I walked to the gun store. I didn't want to go home."[103]

> *"Two things scare me. The first is getting hurt. But that's not nearly as scary as the second, which is losing"*
>
> —Lance Armstrong, former cyclist

Poor decisions can unfortunately have very serious consequences. Consider the tragic death of Jeff Gladney, a cornerback for the Arizona Cardinals, who was only 25 years old. He died on May 30, 2022, in a car crash. According to police reports, the crash happened around 2:30 a.m. in Dallas, Texas. It is believed one vehicle was speeding and clipped a second vehicle from behind. The speeding vehicle then lost control and hit a support beam. A second occupant in the speeding vehicle was also killed; both Gladney and the unidentified occupant were pronounced dead at the scene.[104]

To some athletes, being bad might translate into penalty minutes or technical fouls, while others may be sidelined for the entire game, or suspended for the season. This will significantly impact the athlete's personal and professional brand and damage his negotiation leverage at contract time. If any of the nonconforming, maverick-like, poor sportsmanship behaviors negatively impact the team, or disrupt the functionality of the franchise or league, players can expect to be fined heavily and maybe even kicked out of the sport – banned for life. Needless to say, these consequences can put a chokehold on earnings potential.

A Few Words about Gambling

Your signing bonus was just wired to your bank account and now you're ready to have some fun. Want to make your exciting life more over-the-top? Ready to test your skills at blackjack? What about that primetime parlay play? Like other entertainment, gambling is a fun way to escape the stressors of life, but if not done in moderation, it can become addictive with catastrophic consequences. There are ways you can gamble responsibly, have a good time, and not jeopardize your financial future. Be mindful to preset your gambling limit, realize the house will eventually win, don't get a cash advance from your high-interest credit card to gamble, never ask for a house or casino credit, and know when to say *enough*.

If you get caught up and find yourself gambling excessively and overextending yourself financially, this will impact your reputation in your sphere of influence, and there's a good chance you could deplete your savings long before you retire. If you become known as someone who has a gambling problem, you may have difficulty signing with a team or a sponsor, and the prospects of earning good money after you retire from sports will probably be limited. Research on athletes and compulsive gambling is pretty much nonexistent. However, elite athletes may be more vulnerable than the general public to excessive wagering / gambling when examining signs of compulsive gambling: high levels of dopaminergic energy, unreasonable expectations of winning, extremely competitive personality traits, and distorted optimism. These are also traits of a highly competitive elite athlete.

Drugs, alcohol, and gambling are all vices that have ruined the lives of many athletes. No one is immune to the consequences of poor and misguided decision-making; even the most talented and decorated pro athletes have succumbed to these vices, which inhibit their ability to perform at their peak readiness state, thus limiting their financial potential. John Daly, winner of the 1991 PGA tournament, has been very open about his gambling addiction. He even wrote a book about it: *My Life In & Out of the Rough,* with Glen Waggoner. He says, "I was shocked. I thought it [total gambling loses] might have been $20–25 [million]. I had no idea it was $55–57 million. Nah, it was crazy."[105] Daly also shared in an interview on *In Depth with Graham Bensinger,* "I love the action. I love the adrenaline going in there,"[106] speaking of the reason why he gambled so excessively.

According to Michael Franzese, a gambler, former member of the Mafia, and now public speaker, the gambling addiction is real: "Every gambler will tell you the same thing. 'Whenever I want to quit, I can stop. No problem.' But that's not true."[107]

In an interview on the syndicated TV interview show *In Depth with Graham Bensinger,* Graham asked Charles Barkley, former NBA power forward, what he liked about gambling. Barkley answered, "Winning. It's exciting to win money. It always sucks when you lose, but it's a great feeling when you win." Later during the same interview, Barkley admitted that he lost more millions than he won over the years when he was addicted to gambling. "I've won a million dollars probably four or five times in a single day. But I've lost a lot more millions in a single day. No question it got out of hand."[108]

Phil Mickelson admitted to gambling that was "reckless" and "embarrassing" in an interview with *Sports Illustrated* Morning Read's

Bob Harig after addressing an accusation of him losing more than $40 million in a four-year span. "My gambling got to a point of being reckless and embarrassing," Mickelson said. "I had to address it. And I've been addressing it for a number of years. And for hundreds of hours of therapy. It was just a number of poor decisions."[109]

NBA basketball legend Michael Jordan, arguably the athlete with the most profitable professional brand, was the first NBA player to become a billionaire.[110] It's no secret he loves to gamble. Many gambling stories were swirling around after the ESPN Films and Netflix co-produced documentary series *The Last Dance* aired in 2020. One such story, retold on the documentary by former NBA player Antoine Walker, shared that a 36-hour gambling spree nearly lost him and Jordan $1 million. In a 1993 interview with Connie Chung, featured in *The Last Dance,* Jordan says, "I can stop gambling. I don't have a gambling problem, I have a competition problem, a competition problem."[111] In another interview with Ahmad Rashad in 1993, Jordan describes his gambling as a "hobby." MJ goes on to say "I enjoy it, it's a hobby. If I had a problem, I'd be starving. I'd be hawking this watch, my championship rings, I would sell my house. My wife would have left me, or she'd be starving. I do not have a problem, I enjoy gambling."[112]

Words to the wise:
A gambling addiction is progressive and can have many negative psychological, physical, and social repercussions. Excessive gambling can ruin your financial life—your everything. Period. If you cannot afford to lose, then you can't be like Mike.

"People do not decide their futures, they decide their habits and their habits decide their futures."
—Frederick M. Alexander, actor and author

Reason 36

Making Mental Health an Afterthought

> *"At the end of the day, we're not just entertainment.*
> *We're humans, and there are things going on*
> *behind the scenes that we're also*
> *trying to juggle. . . ."[113]*
>
> —Simone Biles, speaking on mental health of
> athletes at the 2020 Tokyo Olympics

People know your name but not your entire story. They read about your accomplishments, but they don't know what you've been through. While some may think you are doing a terrible job being you, you also struggle with doing what is best for yourself. Sometimes you feel empty and disrespected. You've heard the comedic fodder on late-night talk shows, you've seen the memes on social media about some not-so-wise things elite athletes have done that jeopardized their athletic careers, and you try to drown out the noises. Inhale. Exhale. Those who made bad decisions, you included are entitled to grace, even a mulligan. Give yourself permission to have the full human experience, the ups and the downs, the good, bad *and* ugly.

You know self-care is critically important. If you don't take care of yourself, who will? Sometimes you have to do what's best for you and your health, not necessarily what's best for everyone else. You've heard the popular slogan **"Health is wealth."** By taking care of yourself and fiercely guarding your mental and physical health, you not only improve your competitiveness, but you can also extend your playing days and increase your career earnings well beyond the average competitor.

The saying goes *What doesn't kill you will make you stronger.* Well, this is not entirely true. Adversity is a part of the human experience and, if dealt with properly, can make you stronger. But according to Dr. Lieberman in his book *The Molecule of More*, you first need to garner the courage to prepare for and embrace adversity before it hits, otherwise it could crush you, spiraling into depression or, at worst, suicide.[114] Today's pro athletes face unprecedented pressure, not just to perform but having to navigate and process the love-hate posts on social media by fans and haters, to flawlessly execute a personal branding campaign, and to handle sophisticated financial matters without having the proper know-how and experience. It can be a tall order and can overwhelm.

Dealing with these pressures is where sport psychology comes in. According to the Association for Applied Sport Psychology (AASP), the goal of sport psychology is to "facilitate optimal involvement, performance, and enjoyment in sport and exercise."[115] Since the pandemic, high-profile athletes have publicly disclosed decisions they've made to prioritize their mental health. Stakeholders in the sport community are partnering with these outspoken athletes to ignite an unprecedented movement to shine a spotlight on what was previously a taboo topic.

This collaboration has triggered an important shift in the narrative of mental health in sports. According to an article co-written by Alyson Meister, professor of leadership and organizational behavior, these courageous athletes have "increased the awareness of the numerous career dynamics that pose mental health risks to athletes: unsustainable expectations for perfection and constant improvement, enormous public pressure to win, pervasive demand to outwork or outlast an opponent, and relatively short career spans that can end in the blink of an eye due to injury."[116]

> *"It's interesting when you have an injury [that is seen], it's a lot different when you can't see it and somebody doesn't know what's going on outside the lines. Everybody is going through something. Success is not immune to depression."[117]*
>
> —Kevin Love, five-time NBA All-Star power forward

Is vulnerability a weakness? I believe we all have some level of mental dis-alignment; many of us fall somewhere on the spectrum. Mental health plays an important role in how decisions are made. Study after study show stressful experiences make it harder for people to be rational, leading to impulsivity and risky decision-making. Substance abuse, mental stress, anxiety, and depression in the elite athletic ecosystem have been well documented. Emotional reactions to stressful situations can drain an athlete's physical and mental resources and negatively impact his performance. If you are carrying the weight of unresolved mental issues, it's going to be difficult to make the best decisions about many important life issues, including money.

When asked if the sport community thinks athletes are soft for sharing their mental health struggles, Kevin Love responded, "That's such a tired statement. I've put my time into the league. To be in the NBA, you're not soft. That's tired and outdated. Actually, in the end, is probably for me, it was the best thing I did."[118] There's still exist a stigma associated with mental health.

Solomon Thomas of the NFL New York Jets says this about suffering in silence, "Stigma is still pretty strong. That's the one reason I didn't start to speak right away about my depression, about my journey. I was afraid about what fans would think; if my teammates would think I am soft."[119]

To help combat this stigma, the NBPA created a Mental Health & Wellness Department for its players. The vision as stated on their website is *"We believe that mental health is at the core of maintaining balance between a player's professional, business, personal, family, and spiritual lives. Our goal is to establish a safe place to assist NBA players to uncover the essence of who they are and to achieve excellence."*[120]

> *"Ask for help not because you're weak, but because you want to remain strong."*[121]
>
> —Les Brown, motivational speaker

If you feel that the pressure becomes too great, consider hiring a mind/thought coach or a sports psychologist to help you develop coping skills when stress creeps in or life gets out of balance, to keep a solid emotional equilibrium and keep a positive outlook on life. Having a mind/thought coach may be just as important as having a strength and conditioning coach. A good mind/thought coach or sports psychologist can help with confidence, composure, imagery, focus, goal-setting, pre-performance routines, accepting constructive and non-constructive criticism, and mindfulness. They can help you focus on the things you can control, and dimmish or eliminate thoughts about things you cannot control. Additionally, at some point, you might need help with recovering from an injury, a changing role on the team, team relationships, coach personality challenges, personal issues, family dynamics, career transition, and identity issues after the sports career is over. Strong mental and physical health helps you to maximize your financial potential thereby creating an enviable lifestyle during your professional career and in retirement.

> *"One small crack does not mean that you are broken, it means that you were put to the test, and you didn't fall apart."*
>
> —Linda Poindexter, former episcopal priest

Words to the wise:
A mental edge can bring a winning one.

CHAPTER 6

Dealing with the Law, Including Tax Law

Sprint to the Cliff

You already know that alcohol, drugs, and gambling are all vices that have ruined the lives of many athletes. No one is immune to the consequences of poor decision-making. Even the most talented and most decorated pro athletes have succumbed to these vices, which inhibit their ability to perform at their peak readiness state, thus limiting their financial potential. But what happens to the elite athlete when his irresponsible behavior crosses the line into illegal activities?

Clinical psychologists and criminal researchers point to narcissism as a major contributing factor why athletes engage in criminal activities; some engage in criminal activity just for the thrill of it. Similar findings apply to high-profile public officials, politicians, and business leaders who have been outed for criminal acts. Some athletes may feel that they are invincible or untouchable by the legal system due to their professional status, or that the rules for appropriate behavior do not apply to them. Some even argue that it was the pressure of the profession that made them engage in illegal activities and others may attribute it to CTE, a progressive brain condition. In contrast, a small percentage of elite athletes display bad/illegal behavior because they may not be aware that their actions are illegal, perhaps due to cognitive immaturity or by mistake.

It's a fair observation that some athletes appear not to have the same consequences as "regular Joes" if found guilty of engaging in illegal activities, but a good number suffer serious consequences and are financially ruined as a result of their behavior. Former New England Patriot Aaron Hernandez was 27 years old when he was arrested and charged with murder. He was immediately released by the Patriots. He died by suicide in prison while serving time for first-degree murder.[122] Quarterback Michael Vick pleaded guilty to a federal felony charge related to running a dogfighting ring and served 21 months in federal prison. Vick was 27 years old at the time of his arrest and was once the highest-paid player in the NFL.[123] Michael Phelps, a 23-time gold medalist, faced media scrutiny and lost sponsorships after a video surfaced showing him taking a hit of what appeared to be marijuana from a bong at a house party.[124] (Recreational use was illegal at the time.) Very recently, 18 former NBA players were charged in a $4 million healthcare scheme defrauding the NBA's health and welfare benefit plan,[125] claiming fictitious medical and dental expenses for reimbursement. The case is still pending as of this book's publication.

Rookies and other newbies to the professional sporting community are asked to make lots of adjustments. Turning the "age of majority" and being thrown into the limelight can be a bit daunting for some young athletes. All but three states consider young people to be responsible legal persons at age 18 and having graduated from high school. The state exceptions are Delaware (age 19), Mississippi (age 21), and Nebraska (age 19). At the age of majority, athletes leaving the protective and watchful eye of their high school and college handlers find themselves in an environment of new rights—and new responsibilities. Entering adulthood and the real work world and celebrating new freedoms with access to a boatload of money, newbies are quickly ushered into adulting.

Lions, tigers, and bears—oh yes, there are a myriad of beastly laws facing the newly crowned millionaire: business and breach of contract laws, sports agency laws, landlord/tenant laws, mortgage covenants, paternity statutes, and of course criminal justice laws (to name a few). In most cases, if you are under 18, criminal matters are handled through the juvenile and domestic court systems, in which penalties are typically not very severe, and the records are sealed. But once you are 18 (or the age of majority in your state), you are fully responsible for any criminal laws you break, just like any other adult.

A thorough review of the law as it relates to young male athletes is not the scope of this book. I simply want to make the point that, as you become of legal age, there is a dramatic change regarding your responsibility as a law-abiding citizen. As the wife of a retired police officer, and having raised three alpha male children, I have been well schooled on legal issues facing this segment of the population. Suffice to say that as a young professional athlete, you may have a target on your back. You need to be careful and diligent about following rules set by the authorities. Know and obey laws, and don't go looking for trouble. Simply put, there are things you can't do, places you shouldn't be, and people you shouldn't hang out with. Period. In the wealth-building game, few things are more important than a strong untainted personal brand and a solid professional reputation.

> *"No man is above the law and no man is below it: nor do we ask any man's permission when we ask him to obey it."*
>
> —Theodore Roosevelt

Reason 37

Catching Charges

Run-ins with the law can change your professional trajectory in an epic way. One moment you are flying high as a respected member of an elite sports community and making a lot of money. The next moment, after a series of poor decisions, you are facing serious legal issues, and potentially out of a job you love with little chance of reputation and career redemption. Pro athletes may have more athletic talent than the average person, but this generally does not help them stay out of trouble with the law. They are no less vulnerable than the rest of the 99 percenters.

Criminal activity by professional athletes runs the gamut: minor traffic violations, speeding, shoplifting, vandalism, marijuana possession, marijuana possession with the intent to distribute, crack cocaine distribution, trespassing, disorderly conduct, resisting arrest, assault of a family member, solicitation of prostitutes, public intoxication, drunk driving, DWI, DUI, possession of a controlled substance, felony gun possession, harassment, bribery, criminal mischief, strong arm robbery, gambling violations, fraud, battery/domestic abuse, illegal handgun/weapon charges, aggravated assault with a deadly weapon, sexual assault, rape, hit and run resulting in death of the victim, conspiracy to commit murder for hire, manslaughter, conspiracy to commit murder by hiring a hitman, and murder. This list of illegal behaviors is by no means all inclusive.

According to a slick interactive visual using the NFL crime database, currently 7% of active NFL players have been arrested,[126] which is lower than the arrest rate for the whole of the U.S. population. DUI, domestic violence, and assault and battery are the most common crimes perpetrated by professional athletes in the NFL—and these generally take place in the off-season, but not always.[127] On November 3, 2021, according to arrest records, Raiders wide receiver Henry James Ruggs III was driving 156 mph on a city street with a blood-alcohol content twice Nevada's legal limit before his car slammed into the rear of another vehicle.[128] He is accused of being involved in a fiery crash that killed a woman.

A host of professional athletes have been convicted of drug charges or related crimes while actively competing or soon after retiring. Some cases a decade old are still being fought in the court system, including various drug trafficking, drug dealing, and drug possession cases.

Pro athletes have a lot of collateral considerations when facing a formal charge of a crime or a criminal conviction, including but not limited to league contractual complications, the need to minimize publicity surrounding the legal claims, and managing issues related to paid endorsements. Consequences include instant removal from the team and indefinite suspension, without pay. If you are serving time in jail or subject to or awaiting jail time, you can't suit up for competition—ergo you don't get paid. A sad truth is, with no financial resources to live on, some pro athletes resort to illegal activities out of desperation after retiring. Don't let this be you.

Words to the wise:
Just don't do it.

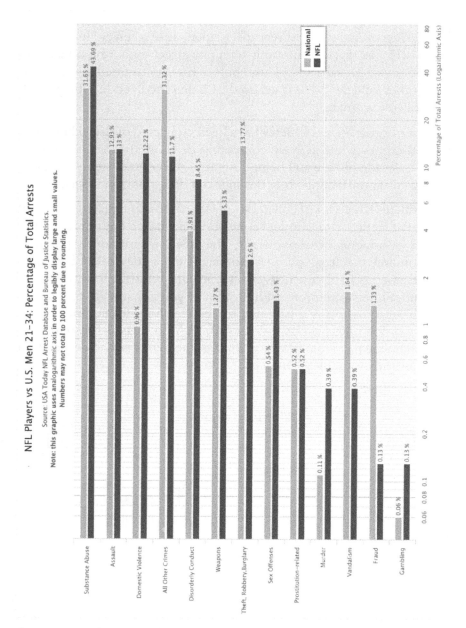

NFL Players vs U.S. Men 21–34: Percentage of Total Arrests

Source: USA Today NFL Arrest Database and Bureau of Justice Statistics.

Note: this graphic uses analogarithmic axis in order to legibly display large and small values. Numbers may not total to 100 percent due to rounding.

Percentage of Total Arrests (Logarithmic Axis)

National
NFL

Category	National	NFL
Substance Abuse	31.65 %	43.69 %
Assault	12.93 %	13 %
Domestic Violence	0.96 %	12.22 %
All Other Crimes	31.32 %	11.7 %
Disorderly Conduct	3.91 %	8.45 %
Weapons	1.27 %	5.33 %
Theft, Robbery, Burglary	13.77 %	2.6 %
Sex Offenses	0.54 %	1.43 %
Prostitution-related	0.52 %	0.52 %
Murder	0.11 %	0.39 %
Vandalism	1.64 %	0.39 %
Fraud	1.33 %	0.13 %
Gambling	0.06 %	0.13 %

Go to my website to get the most current chart published by Crime in the NFL | CNSMaryland.org LyndaPaul.com

Reason 38

State Domicile and Saving Tax Dollars

It's happening all around us, quietly. People are trying to find ways to pay fewer taxes so they can enjoy a higher percentage of the money they earn. What if I told you that saving tax dollars is immediately possible if you relocate to one of the few states that has a zero-income tax? How do I know? Because I recently relocated to a state that has no income taxes. At the time of this printing, nine states in the U.S. don't have an income tax: Alaska, Florida, Nevada, New Hampshire, South Dakota, Tennessee, Texas, Washington, and Wyoming. New Hampshire, however, taxes interest and dividends. Even if you can reduce the amount of your state income taxes, please know you will still be responsible for paying federal taxes.

For simplicity, I do not plan to be very technical in this chapter. My purpose is to give you a few ideas for how you may be able to save money on taxes legally. You should consult with your tax professional to inquire how you can incorporate tax-saving strategies in your overall financial plan.

It is not uncommon for pro athletes to have more than one personal residence in different states. But which state is his legal residence? Americans can have more than one state residency but can only have one legal domicile—which is the basis upon which states use to impose taxes on your income. Many people think about the 183-day rule when determining if you are a legal resident—and if you qualify for the favorable tax treatment of a particular state. The "six months plus one day" rule is important, but it is not the determining factor if you are a legal statutory resident of a particular state. The domicile rule is the determinate factor for most states to assign your legal residency. Domicile means that by law you are physically present in the state with an intent of remaining in the state permanently for the foreseeable future. In other words, your intent to be known as a permanent resident is the most important factor. If after discussing it with your tax advisor you plan to relocate to a no-income-tax state, it's important that you do whatever is necessary to gather evidential matter to protect your legal status if you are ever challenged in a state audit.

Here are a few ways you can prove your intent to be a permanent legal resident of a particular state, giving you rights to favorable tax treatments just like other legal residents of that state:

- Purchase real property/a residence
- Change your driver's license/register your vehicles
- Change your voter registration
- Change your address on your federal tax returns
- Get a new bank account in that state or change the address on your existing account
- Find a physician in your new state and document visits
- Join a church or synagogue in your new community
- Engage in community events
- Get a library card
- Change your will and other state-relevant estate-planning documents

What does a state tax savings look like in dollar terms? If you consider a move from California, known as a high-tax state, to Florida, a state with no income tax, how can a change in state domicile benefit you from a tax standpoint? Let's say, for illustrative purposes, you receive a $5M dollar signing bonus. Keeping things simple, using Cali's progressive tax rate of 12.3%, filing single, your state income tax bill would be approximately $615,000. If you lived in Florida, you would pay $0 in state income taxes, since Florida is one of the states that has no state income tax. These tax savings look attractive but be mindful there may be other tax caveats or state residency issues to consider.

Recently, NBA guard Stephen Curry reportedly signed a four-year, $215,353,664 guaranteed contract with the Golden State Warriors that will span from the 2023 season to the conclusion of the 2026 season.[129] The Golden State Warriors play their homes games at the Chase Center in San Francisco, California, and they also play many of their in-league games in California, a high-income tax state. While I do not profess to know much about Mr. Curry's tax situation or his legal domicile, I am certain he and his tax advisors have structured his contract to mitigate the tax bite such that California income taxes will have little impact on his ability to live a comfortable lifestyle. This may not be true for other pro athletes who are domiciled in California.

Tiger Woods acknowledged years ago when he first turned pro that he left California for Florida because of the difference in state income tax obligation.[130] Woods, who reportedly earned $56.4 million in 2012, kept roughly $7.5 million of income he otherwise would have owed to the state of California. Of course you want to pay the taxes you are legally obligated to pay, but the more you can keep of your income, the better off you'll be, financially speaking.

> *"You don't get any special treatment from the government from overpaying taxes."*[131]
>
> —Zack Miller, former NFL tight end

Words to the wise:
And now you know why I moved 5 years ago. You're welcome.

Reason 39

The Dreaded "Jock Tax"

In 2017, according to many sources, LeBron James was the highest paid athlete in the U.S., and the second-highest-paid athlete in the world, with an estimated $86 million dollars from salary and endorsement deals.[132] When tax time rolled around, LeBron and his financial team undoubtedly had a myriad of federal tax forms to process and an estimated 21 state tax returns to file in the states where he played and earned compensation, making the completed tax return easily hundreds of pages deep.

All around the world, when media broadcasts the contract amounts and signing bonuses pro athletes sign for, the gross amount, not net, is usually published. When said out loud, the gross contract amounts sound like a lot of money, but even pro athletes forget that they actually do not get the reported figures. They get the net amount. After taxes, agent commissions, and so forth, the net amount is substantially less— maybe less than 50% of the published figure. As a well-paid professional athlete, taxes are one of your biggest expenses, so time and effort should be invested to make sure you pay your legally required amount, but not one penny more. Of course, no one expects you to know all this tax jargon, but since you are reading this book, you now know what questions to ask your financial/tax team during free agency.

> *"The first mistake is, people say, 'Okay, I've got $11 million' [according to the contract]. You've got five [million dollars after taxes] over four years."*
>
> —Josh Childress, sixth pick of the 2004 NBA draft, who signed a four-year rookie contract worth $11.7 million

Athletes can earn tens of thousands of dollars per year in taxable income when they travel out of state for a game or endorsement gigs. This is an attractive source of tax revenue for state governments. The "jock tax" is the colloquially named income tax levied against visitors to a city or state who earn money in that jurisdiction. The "jock tax" generally relates to state taxes, but a few cities and counties also levy taxes based on the earnings of professional athletes who visit and play in their city. In addition to the visiting athletes, the "jock tax" is also imposed on other employees of the team who travel with the players, including coaches, doctors, trainers, and even team chefs. In cases of an individual sport like tennis or boxing, the pro athlete and their paid entourage are subject to this "jock tax."

While this state/county/city tax can be applied to other nonresident, itinerant professionals working in a particular city or state, the "jock tax" is often levied against very wealthy and high-profile individuals, entertainers, and public speakers, not just professional athletes. But why so much attention on pro athletes? They are an easy target. It's just easier for states' tax revenue departments to track high-profile individuals versus the many other visiting individuals who do business on an itinerant basis. Pro athletes' travel schedules and contracted salaries are public and easily obtained.

Not everyone is happy with this added tax burden. Recently there have been some legal challenges to this "jock tax" to ensure that professional athletes are not subjected to unequal treatment due to their economic status. One ongoing legal challenge was filed by a trio of professional athletes and the players' associations of Major League Baseball, the National Football League, and the National Hockey League, all of which allege that the City of Pittsburgh's "jock tax" is unconstitutional. Pittsburgh allegedly charges nonresident visiting athletes 3% of their taxable "earned income," which includes salaries, wages, and bonus earned while visiting the city of Pittsburgh, but charges only 1% of taxable "earned income" to its residents.[133] This appears to be a clear case on tax discrimination and against the U.S. Constitution, which ensures that no single group (like professional athletes) can be targeted to pay higher taxes. Stay tuned.

> *"...but in this world nothing can be said to be certain, except death and taxes."*
>
> —Benjamin Franklin

Words to the wise:

A knowledgeable tax team is clutch.

CHAPTER 7

Groupies and Tinder Love

DM Me

We are all looking for love. But why is it so difficult to find it? And keep it? Many online dating sites exist to help eager seekers find a suitable match. The platforms vary in terms of targeted demographics, anonymity, and effectiveness of match-making algorithms, but the one thing all dating sites have in common is the attraction of enthusiastically lonely individuals seeking personal encounters. Whether for a short-term physical hookup or long-lasting romantic engagement with a possibility of marriage, dating sites are set up to curate a dating experience like no other. Surveys by users of online dating platforms credit sites for (1) expanding options to meet people outside of their immediate circle of acquaintances, (2) allowing seekers to evaluate potential matches before meeting them in person, (3) connecting likeminded people, (4) eliminating or reducing the awkwardness of a first encounter, and (5) making meeting people easier—all mostly positive commentary. The downside is many suitors make gross misrepresentations of their physical attributes.

Your schedule is busy with games/matches/races/field competitions, practice, training, team meetings, PR obligations, traveling, and self-care routines. It's just not convenient to take the traditional dating routes. The Tinder dating app was created for such a person in your dating predicament; it's meetup 101. "Swipe right" to accept or "swipe left" to reject. At one point, Tinder was registering about one billion daily "swipes" and reported that users logged in to the app on average 11 times a day.[134] Because pro athletes travel around the country during the season, Tinder has become one of the best ways for pro athletes to get familiar with a new city and potentially a search for Ms. Right— well, at least for the night. During the pandemic in 2020, Tinder reported usage was up more than 20% and boasted that the dating site had more than 3 billion swipes in a single day for the first time on Saturday, March 28, 2020.[135]

You have high value in the dating market, and you know it. As a healthy heterosexual male pro athlete dating prospect, there are a lot of women all over the world looking to date you and doing whatever it takes to snag a bonified, well-paid beau like you. NBA Hall of Famer Dennis Rodman may have said it best in an interview on *Dateline* with Stone Phillips: "It's like a meat market. You got your fresh choice, you got this, you got that, you got your cuts here, you got all kinds of cuts."[136] It's exciting to meet new people and enjoy the dating experience, but if a personal relationship or the ending of one is not managed properly, your personal and professional brand can be negatively impacted. If you become a party to a lawsuit by a former lover, a victim of an extortion plot or exploitation, or a father of unplanned children thrown in the middle of baby mama drama, this can lead to a substantial decrease in your professional status with devasting financial ramifications.

Many pro athletes end up marrying their high school or college sweethearts, but despite this eventuality, women still jockey for position to hit the dating game jackpot. The hopeful payoff of this "man-catching" mission if successful? A good time with a physically attractive, well-groomed pro athlete who has the financial resources to give her a dating experience unmatched by other suitors, and possibly a proposal for marriage. After the wooing, is an ensuing wedding a panacea? For her, a wedding may be followed by a lifetime of wealth either from a long-term marriage relationship or a lucrative spousal support arrangement after the divorce. That's the ticket. Or is it?

Is there such a thing as happily ever after? The divorce rate for pro athletes is estimated at between 60% to 80%,[137] much higher than the rate for the general public. The sport season dominates. Due to the high stress and extraordinary pressure of the sport grind, marital issues are seldom brought up during the season, and generally are not addressed until retirement.

Halfsies: A Word about Prenups

The idea of forfeiting half of your fortune to a sizable alimony should give you reason to **pause** and think about how you can prevent this from happening to you. A prenuptial agreement (prenup) protects you from the worst-case scenario. When designed properly, a prenup safeguards your assets, contract income, and earnings from endorsements and sponsorship deals. Also, a good prenup shields intimate details of your personal life and final financial settlements from talking heads in the media with confidentiality language and a non-disclosure agreement (NDA).

Warning: Having a prenup drawn up during the engagement period of the relationship may affect the intimacy and the courtship. Proceed delicately.

An interesting tidbit: Even after the headlines of Tiger Woods's trail of marital infidelities, many family law attorneys agree the culture of sexual infidelity is so pervasive in professional sports that it's become commonplace; all pro athletes need to stay educated about the nuance of sexual infidelity/ensuing divorce, even to the point of including a special cheating clause, called a "bad boy provision," in prenuptial agreements.

Carla Lundblade, a licensed clinical therapist who specializes in sports and celebrity culture, created a 10-point system of managing the high-profile lifestyle:

The "Lundblade System"[138]

1. Seek out professional investment specialists early on in your career.
2. Don't give in to showing off your new "richness" to teammates, fans, or loved one.
3. Never hire friends, family, or former coaches to manage your finances. Hire for expertise, not relationship.
4. Check the background of your financial advisers. Many have questionable pasts, or worse, criminal backgrounds directly related to money. Also, watch for people over-charging you for services.
5. Effectively handle and manage the flood of new people entering your life; don't let them handle you.

6. Limit paternity. Choose love relationships carefully and reduce the chance of having unplanned children. For some athletes, child-support payments are their largest payouts.
7. Don't get married too young and don't think marrying your hometown sweetheart or someone who knew you before the success is always a smart decision. It's not.
8. Draw up a good prenuptial when you do get married. Not all prenuptials are created equal, so make sure yours is solid.
9. Don't get divorced. The divorce rate among professional athletes is 60–80 percent, and almost all happen in retirement. The athlete's peak earning periods are usually long over by this time and making the same amount of money as he once did is virtually impossible.
10. Draw up a will. In steps 1 through 9 you've protected and nurtured the security of your bright financial future, so do the same for your family just in case you're not there to take care of them.

Reason 40

Baby Mama, Financial Drama

There she is. That's your type. You see her out of the corner of your eye as you sip your refreshing beverage. She's got mad cake and the full package, and you'd like to get to know her *better*. You get up from your table as if you're heading to the bar to get her attention, then you make a beeline toward the hottie. You give her your number, invite her to your next game, and hint of a rendezvous after the game, to join you for dinner. It's on. This could be the beginning of something special— or something else.

The relationship is going well, then you hear those unexpected words: "I just got the results and we're pregnant."

"How did that happen?" you ask yourself over and over, dumbfounded, as you attempt to concoct some quick understanding in your mind. "Damn!" Some professional athletes are well known for making moves on the court, field, or ice, but others are better known for making babies. Many have gone on the record and said their child-support payments are causing them to go broke. Others have abandoned their legal obligations and are being sued by their baby's mama for unpaid child support, risking large penalties and even jail time for failure to pay support owed. Sexual misadventures can lead to unplanned fatherhood, an unwanted toxic relationship with the child's mother, and financial mayhem. The best way to handle the baby mama drama problem is to not create one.

Coming in hot. Does the sportin' lifestyle encourage irresponsible behavior? Physiologically speaking, pro athletes are at their sexual energy peak when they start their professional careers. This new journey is an exciting time of physical expression. With a robust libido, substantial financial resources, and seemingly unlimited choices of seductive dating options, newly famous pro athletes amplify their strong appetite for sexual encounters—and lots of them.

Consequently, the more sexual partners, the more vulnerable you are to unintended pregnancies and subsequent paternity actions, including lawsuits for child support. Do some women target athletes in hopes of having their children and then living off the generous child support? Perhaps, but it takes two to tango. The correlation is obvious: The number of baby mamas a professional athlete has is a good indication that he will experience some financial stress after he retires from the sport. High child-support payments, spousal support/alimony, and other financial benefits subjugated by the baby's mama are a sure way to end up broke.

Why does it seem child-support payments are high for pro athletes' offsprings compared to payments for other children? If the paternity issues arise during his active playing days, his high income is used in the child-support review process to calculate the support payments. Here's the rub: Over the 18 years of child support, much of the cash payout takes place *after* retiring from the sport career. The years of high sports earnings have ended and now these athletes are living on savings, pensions, and income generated by a second career, which in most cases is quite a bit less than the income he enjoyed during his playing days.

You can see how this ill-timed payment scheme plays out. It is not an ideal situation, to make now and pay later. Having a child with someone after a Tinder swipe doesn't just place you in child-support payment confinement for 18 years, but having children changes your life forever. (That's *FOR-EV-ER,* in my slow-mo play voice from *The Sandlot.*)

Many paternity cases are settled quietly out of respect for the child's privacy, and therefore do not get much media attention, but some high-profile cases inundate headlines around the globe:

Evander Holyfield, former boxing great, is reported to have fathered 11 kids with six different women.[139] At one point, it was rumored that he was paying more than $500,000 per year in child support. BTW, some of his kids are now aging out of the system and starting sport careers of their own.

Dwight Howard, former NBA big man, is reported to have fathered five kids with five different women.[140] At one point, it was rumored that he was paying more than $50,000 per month in child-support.

Travis Henry, former NFL running back, is reported to have fathered 11 children with 10 different women.[141] He is reportedly being sued by some of his baby mamas after falling behind on his child-support legal obligations. Henry's child-support obligation is estimated to be $170,000 per year.

Antonio Cromartie, former NFL cornerback, is reported to have 14 kids with eight different women and at one time was reportedly paying $336,000 per year in child support.[142] Antonio's life has been chronicled in a reality TV show called *The Cromarties*.[143]

Blake Griffin, NBA small forward, was recently in the news with a very public breakup with his ex-fiancée, who is the mother of his two children. It was originally rumored that Griffin was ordered to pay $258,000 per month in child support. Details are hard to get unless one has access to child-support court documents. Griffin did share, when pressed, that with the paternity lawsuit he pays for a five-bedroom home in Manhattan Beach, California, for his former fiancée and his two children. After the smoked cleared, it was later reported that the child-support amount was not $258,000 per month, but $32,000 per month, which adds up to $384,000 per year.[144]

> *Sidebar: Professional athletes are not the only ones who might experience baby mama drama. Elon Musk, founder of Tesla and SpaceX, is in a class of his own and might take home the prize when all has been said and done in the baby-making/child-support recreational sport.*
>
> *Musk, who was crowned by Bloomberg in July 2022 as the world's richest man,[145] had his 10th child born in December 2021. Elon has children with three different women. His first child tragically died at the age of 10 weeks. Musk revealed a reason for his baby-making prowess in recent articles and implied he might not be finished: "A collapsing birth rate is the biggest danger civilization faces by far."[146]*
>
> *After publicly acknowledging in the summer of 2022 that he has twins who were born in November 2021, Elon tweeted, "Doing my best to help the underpopulation crisis."[147] According to TikTok posts, Musk's baby-making abilities are in high demand (#ElonMuskIsHot).*

How Much Does it Cost to Raise a Child?

According to the U.S. Department of Agriculture, taking inflation into consideration, in 2022, it will take approximately $286,000 to raise a child until age 18, and another $141,300 for a four-year college degree, including books, supplies, housing, and daily living expenses.[148] Aside from the love and moral support of children, child support is real—and costs real dollars. The good news in all of this is each additional child costs less, thanks to economies of scale, *unless* you have a different mama for each of your children.

According to family law information at nolo.com, each state has a formula for calculating child support, but there are federal guidelines.[149] The courts overwhelmingly agree that parents have an obligation to support their children, at the standard of living enjoyed by one or both parents, especially if you have a dad who makes a lot of money in professional sports. The biggest factor in calculating child support is how much the parents earn. Some states consider both parents' income, but other states consider only the income of the noncustodial parent. The percentage of time that each parent spends with the children is another important factor.

But what if the noncustodial parent is a pro athlete making millions of dollars? This can throw off the generally accepted support computations. In cases in which monthly income is above a certain amount—as is the case of many pro athletes and other high wage earners—the child-support computation is left to the discretion of the court/judge. Because of this discretion, the dollar amount of awards varies significantly on a case-by-case basis, as many other factors are taken into consideration. The judge weighs unique circumstances related to a pro athlete's high initial income for a relatively short duration, gross versus after-tax net income due to the high tax burden, and a presumption that income can decrease suddenly due to an injury or the possibility of being cut from the team, or a contract or endorsement deal not renewed.

The child should enjoy the standard of living that would have existed had the parties not separated, implying that the child should share in the parent's good fortune. The child's life, including lifestyle upgrades, should reasonably reflect that of the child's parents, especially the lifestyle of the dad, who happens to be a well-paid professional athlete. Of paramount concern in determining the proper standard of living is the *best interest of the child*. Parents who fail or refuse to pay judge-approved child support can go to jail and pay thousands of dollars in fines and penalties—on top of the child support they owe.

If the noncustodial parent is a deadbeat parent, the judge can issue a wage assignment/garnishment that results in an automatic deduction from their paycheck. Additionally, the court may allow the custodial parent to levy or place a lien on the deadbeat's bank accounts, stocks, or other personal and business property, including real estate.

What is baby mama drama on steroids? When the baby's mama uses the child as a pawn to manipulate the dad, uses child-support funds for her own personal use, or limit visitations unless more support is agreed to, thereby holding the child's right to engage with their dad as hostage.

The child support paid by the pro athletes is generally for the well-being and needs of the child(ren), and not to be used by the baby mama for her personal purposes and self-indulgence. In acrimonious baby mama situations, the child can end up as collateral damage or, worse, collaterally damaged.

Words to the wise:
Poor or reckless decisions made while actively earning lots of money can negatively and substantially impact cash flow after you retire from the sport. Heed the warning of self-protection: BYOC. ***Wrap it before you tap it,*** because your pull-out game might be weak.

Photo credit Adobe Photos

Aren't they adorable – Cha-Ching $$

Reason 41

Divas and Financial Infidelity

When you hear or read the word *infidelity,* you might unconsciously think of marital infidelity, and automatically envision a cheating spouse or partner—and the ensuing divorce proceedings. Professional athletes have a fantastic reputation for cheating while married or in a committed relationship. Marital infidelity, a violation of a couple's sexual exclusivity and trust, is a major stressor for the person who has learned that their spouse or significant other has been unfaithful. This betrayal can be emotionally unstable and financially devastating, as it oftentimes leads to a separation or divorce.

Financial infidelity, a violation of expected behavior involving money, is equally damning to a committed relationship. Financial infidelity is known to activate the same "trust button" in the emotional brain as sexual infidelity; to the body, the negative energy brought about from the betrayal feels the same. This breach of trust creates tension and difficulty in relationships, as the partner feels deeply wounded. Irreconcilable differences with money issues is a leading cause of divorce.[150]

So, how does one engage in this trustbuster? When couples with combined finances lie to each other about money spent, assets owned, and debts accumulated, they are generally engaging in financial infidelity. One spouse or significant other may open a secret credit card and subsequently max out the available balance without their partner's knowledge. Setting up a savings account without the other's knowledge, intentionally hiding a purchase, using a cash bonus to buy big-ticket items, and taking out a personal loan to fund a second lifestyle—in secret, without sharing the information with a spouse or significant other—are examples of financial infidelity. These are all intentional acts to hide and deceive. Money can be a big point of contention between couples, especially if one of the partners is the primary breadwinner and the other a homemaker, which is a very common lifestyle for the married/committed pro athlete and his partner.

Financial infidelity is different from financial irresponsibility. One is intentional betrayal, a true character issue; the other is a lack of financial wisdom. Signs of financial infidelity include discovering charges for gifts for side chicks or side dudes on a secret credit card, a partner taking excessive trips and lying about how they were paid for, finding stuffed shopping bags in the trunk of the car, receiving random calls about outstanding gambling debts, the "cheating" partner always wanting to grab the mail first, a changed password to deny access to account information, or defensiveness when one partner raises questions about declining bank balances.

The true pain comes when the unknowing partner learns their true financial situation is far worse than expected, crushed by lower actual savings and higher debt. This new financial reality leaves the scorned partner asking, "What else don't I know?" When someone lies about something, they will lie about anything. Not recognizing financial infidelity early enough can jeopardized your financial security. If your romantic partner is a diva who engages in financial infidelity, you need to confront this behavior immediately, with gentle prudence. If you are the culpable diva, repent and ask for forgiveness. Committed couples should insist and expect complete transparency in money matters.

Words to the wise:
For exclusive relationships, both partners should take active roles in managing the combined finances. *Financial transparency* is the new term for *financial accountability*.

CHAPTER 8

Paradigm Shift

The Truth

What's the difference between being rich and being wealthy? A rich person has high income from a well-paid job and can afford a big home, fancy cars, and luxury goods. He may have a positive net worth; however, he could also be swimming in debt and on the edge of insolvency. At some point, the high income may evaporate as a result of a series of unfortunate events, including job loss or a disability, and without an adequate financial safety net, the rich person may find himself in financial distress. A wealthy person can afford to buy all the luxury items mentioned above but does not depend on his work income to maintain his standard of living; his intellectual capital and accumulated assets give him the means to sustain his wealth.

Some people see a person driving a fancy car and think he is wealthy and has got it made. We tend to judge by what we see. In contrast, real wealth is not on full display and is generally very quiet. The value we place on money and wealth is interwoven with our overall value system—which helps us to more easily discern what is important and what's not. We learn about money early in life, and as such we created beliefs about money – over time. What are beliefs? Beliefs are thoughts we keep thinking until they become ingrained in our conscious and subconscious mind. A belief can also be an opinion or something that you hold to be true. Beliefs become paradigms—frameworks for how you live your life. But what if those beliefs are limiting? Or are not true? Can these limiting or false beliefs sabotage your financial future or hold you back from realizing your full financial potential? Yes they can.

A paradigm is the way you see things, filtered by the lens you use to look out into the world. Your paradigms are based on your background and psychological modeling, and the belief system you use to process your reality. Some call it social programming, where the subconscious mind strongly influences thinking and behavior. Paradigms affect everything in life. Traditional paradigms are deeply ingrained culturally, and this indoctrination makes it harder to modify paradigms. So, if a paradigm uses your belief system to process reality, and a belief is not a fact, but just a *thought* that we keep thinking, then it seems reasonable to reexamine beliefs that are not serving us and change them, yes? This change or tweak in a belief system is a paradigm shift. An example of a paradigm shift is a change in mindset from *I know it all* to *I know that I do not know it all.* This subtle change in a belief system can help transform your views about learning new things and invite the courage to ask questions. Truth is, professional athletes need to consider paradigm shifts in three areas: spending money, selecting role models and mentors, and saving for or allocating funds to the future.

Spending Money

Values, beliefs, and spending are highly interrelated. Can you identify your beliefs by examining how you spend money? Do you spend money to show people you have money? What if you grew up poor as a child? You might now look at the world through the lens of a poor child living in scarcity. As a newly crowned millionaire, your beliefs may manifest into living an overindulgent lifestyle with a mentality of lack. Maybe you never felt secure, and you learned to be more comfortable buying things to touch and hold for immediate gratification, instead of learning about the wealth-generating potential of intangibles or investing in stocks. It could also mean that you spend as soon as you get your hands on the cash because you are afraid it might be lost or someone in authority might take it away.

Spending more and saving less while focusing on the present may be your paradigm and how you see yourself living your best life. Maybe you splurge or spend more money than you should because of fear, or it's difficult to envision a prosperous future, or you are in search of respect or admiration by using your purchasing power, or you prefer to hang with the Joneses, or you lack self-discipline. These mindsets are scarcity paradigms. If any of these describes you, you might need a new way of thinking about money and spending—a new paradigm.

Selecting Role Models and Mentors

Learning by imitation can be a great way to adopt acceptable behaviors as a new member in the professional sports community. Modeling strong veteran role models accelerates learning. But what if there's a belief that the "bad boy" veterans are the ones to emulate? Maybe the veterans who appear on the surface to be physically superior, emotionally stoic, and financially successful are believed to be the role models to pattern your sports career after? Since there's no real transparency, the truth about character and financial discipline may be hard to uncover. As a young professional, you are asked to adjust and make important decisions early in your career. Determining early what impact you would like to have on your sport and who is/are the best person/people to help you should be on the top of the list. Be intentional.

Consider what you think are solid character traits of a role model, someone worthy of your adulations and emulation. How important are humility, empathy, professionalism, and a commitment to behaving responsibly? Someone who demonstrates personal integrity, is transparent, shows positivity, is honest, and behaves ethically? Do you think someone who is respectful and accepts and embraces the role of a leader would be an ideal role model? Choose role models who already have what you want for yourself. Compare them to other successful people you admire outside your sport. Watch how responsible veterans in your sport spend and handle their money.

Brandon and his mentor, Dickey Simpkins (Chicago Bulls)

There will be pressure placed on you to listen to and follow veterans on *your* team or in *your* sport, but you should ask yourself if those veterans are the right role models for you. Be respectful and find a way to do things your way. Charles Barkley, 13-year NBA veteran, famously said, "I am not a role model."[151] When someone tells you either verbally or by their actions who they are—or are not—believe them. Take the time to find which pro cohort is successful with managing their money and find out why, and don't waste time and money emulating deadbeats.

Five-time Pro Bowl running back Alvin Kamara, who recently signed a $75 million dollar contract extension, might be a role model for other young athletes. The 25-year-old is trying to live in a way that honors his mom. He says, "As a kid, I saw my mom work multiple jobs only to be able to afford the bare essentials."[152] In an interview for Uninterrupted *Kneading Dough* series, he shared that the lesson he learned about hard work from his mom keeps him humble and conscious about living well within his means. Kamara says that after four seasons in the NFL, he has yet to spend any of this football money from either his rookie contract or his recent contract extension. Instead, he lives off the money that he earns doing endorsements.[153]

If you like the way some veterans handle themselves and their money, and they have solid character and honorable reputations, they may be good role models for you. Perhaps you can ask if one of these veterans would consider becoming your mentor.

Saving for or Allocating Funds to the Future

Some young professional athletes who are awarded large rookie contracts may think they do not need to save because they believe the money will keep flowing. Truth is, the money *will* stop flowing, making it imperative to save funds for a secure future. Saving money is a skill, and like other skills you have, it needs to be practiced. If the act of saving was never modeled in your household as a child, it might be a difficult skill to learn—especially now that you have millions—but it's not impossible.

Saving relies more on psychology than the amount you need to save or allocate; mindset is more important than strategy. In his book *The*

Psychology of Money, Morgan Housel defines savings as the gap between your ego and your income and explained why many people with good income save so little: "One of the most powerful ways to increase your savings isn't to raise your income, but to raise your humility."[154] It's in your control to save more. In fact, savings can be created just by *spending less.* If you believe you need to show off your income by spending on stuff, a paradigm shift for you could be *to stop caring so much about what others think about you.*

A career in sports comes with uncertainties. Savings is a hedge against economic unknowns. When your contract is not renewed, savings give you options and let you live life on your terms. Think about money differently, live well below your means, and create a new mindset of having and saving money, not just spending money. Save more now so you can have more options later.

Easy Peasy?

In theory, saving money may be a simple concept, but the truth is, it can be hard. Studies on present bias versus planning for the future show that we prefer to indulge our current self now and *promise* noble choices for our future self, only to break those promises later. When it comes to money, we opt for immediate gratification. Present bias is the tendency to settle for a smaller present reward, like buying a high-ticket item that brings us immediate pleasure, rather than wait for a larger reward in the future. In a sense, we discount the value of the future thing. Our behavior demonstrates our tendency to overvalue immediate rewards, while putting less significance on long-term positive outcomes.

The brain is highly motivated to seek pleasure, *now.* If we desire to save money for an event far off in time like a child's wedding or college education, the brain is believed to make this an abstract thought and the behavior needed is hijacked so we give our focus to the present or near future. We are just more motivated to solve problems that are short-term and in the present moment—a present bias—than those that are long-term. For example, retirement is some mystical event far, far away in a distant time zone, and saving for this event requires great self-control and discipline; a brain hack may be needed to be successful.

Vividly think about your future self and visualize your economic reality after your sport's career has ended. How do you get from here to there? The financial community has come up with two ways to assist in tackling this present bias phenomenon to help make the act of saving a priority: *pay yourself first* and *automatic retirement savings programs.*

The truth is it's time to challenge deeply held beliefs by embracing shifts in the following paradigms: spending behaviors, choosing appropriate role models, saving more, and remembering to delay immediate gratification by doing a brain hack to conquer present bias tendencies. Making small mental adjustments can change your life and give you a path forward to financial prosperity.

> *"The journey of a thousand miles begins with a single step."*
>
> —Lao Tzu

Reason 42

Victims: The Setup

Everybody wants something from you, even if they have to steal it. Being a professional athlete can bring you fortune and fame, money, and prestige, but it can also bring you lots of attention, especially the kind that's unwanted. You are pulled in all kinds of directions by everyone you meet. Some pro athletes are vulnerable because they just don't know what they don't know.

They are unaware of the games played by bad actors to take advantage of and profit off young, naïve athletes. Young professional athletes are exploited by dishonest agents who may have side deals or other conflicts of interest when negotiating contracts, by unscrupulous financial advisors who place them in bad or arcane and illiquid investments with high fees, by greedy private bankers who siphon money from their accounts, by shady business partners who engage in unethical or illegal business dealings, by deceitful dealerships and retailers who upcharge for cars and jewelry, by shameless family members and friends who borrow money and never pay it back, by self-seeking online groups soliciting funds for "charity" scams, by two-faced groupies engaging in cyber extortion, by thirsty mistresses who seek money for silence, and by scheming love interests who get pregnant using lies and deceptive methods. The list can go on and on. Even members of entourages cannot be fully trusted, stealing luxury watches and sports memorabilia while you sleep.

Criminals and thieves go where the money is—and pro athletes have lots. Besides what was mentioned above, pro athletes can become victims of their own unwise behaviors such as being fleeced by the illusion of value: buying the most expensive car on the car lot without negotiating the final price, getting enticed by luxury brands only to spend five times more than a pedestrian brand for a similar product, shelling out twice the going rate for home remodeling, and even paying a healthy premium for grooming/self-care and childcare. To the unschooled and unsuspecting dupe, it can look and feel like a setup, but these enterprising acts by professional con artists and scammers have been going on for decades. It's like a kabuki shuffle. It's time to wake up and become your own advocate by refusing to continue to be comedic fodder for the late-night talk shows and get your financial house in order and keep it in order.

The Hook

It starts early. When a young prodigy reveals his talents to the world and starts to separate himself as athletically superior, an assortment of ravenous pack animals starts to surround the young cub, and with their feral cunningness sharpened by nefarious intentions and experience, they begin their persistent pursuit by attempting to earn the young cub's trust. Advancing from the back door, the relationship appears very innocent, benevolent, and even helpful, giving the cub a false sense of security. Early on it's not very clear who the predators are, as everyone wants to be attentive and show themselves as friendly. But once the sport phenom turns pro, the true predators tighten their grip and increase their efforts to help themselves to the athlete's big payday.

Years later, as the wounded prey heads for the sidelines and hangs up his jersey, he reflects on the totality of his professional sports experience and takes a closer look at his life and personal finances. The financial butchering is complete. Broke and broken. After the pouncing subsides and the clouds clear, the financial carnage is laid out on full public display: a chunk taken here, a nibble there, crumbs everywhere— financial death by a thousand bites. The pro athlete's hope of a secure financial future in retirement has been spectacularly snatched by cunning wolves and rats dressed in slick pinstripe suits. How can you protect yourself from these ravenous fraudsters and ensure you do not succumb to the same fate? How can you stop these animals of prey from ripping into your financial flesh, which can leave you in financial ruins?

A Google search on scams perpetrated against pro athletes returned thousands of articles, court documents, attorney reviews, and even detailed accounts told by pro athletes themselves. Stories upon stories of pro athletes being wronged in just about every way imaginable: Ponzi schemes, embezzlement, skimming, cooking the books, ripping off, pilfering, home invasions, armed robberies, burglaries, bilked out of, burned, signing illegally for a loan, siphoning off, got jacked, shaken down, defrauded, degraded, deluded, identity theft, social media scams, phishing, bamboozled, duped. There have even been incidents when the pro athlete's agent referred his clients to unscrupulous investment scammers and crooks—and stole money by requiring the athletes sign a power of attorney (POA) giving the fraudsters the right to sign documents as their agent-in-fact. (Check out why it's not a good idea to give just anyone your POA – in Reason #5).

> *The stories make me ill. As a mom of a professional athlete, I cannot believe the lengths and depths people go to steal another person's money. Just wrong, sad, and shameful.*

Do some financial advisors steal from their clients? Of course, but it's a small minority. Following are just a few of the high-profile cases in which a "trusted" financial advisor or business associate allegedly stole from their clients and were accused of committing fraud (amounts are unsubstantiated):

Tim Duncan $20MM;[155] Kareem Abdul-Jabbar, $9MM;[156] Mark Sanchez et al $30MM;[157] Bernie Kosar, $20MM,[158] John Elway, $15MM,[159] Mike Tyson, $100MM,[160] Kevin Garnet $77MM,[161] Dennis Rodman, $5.7MM.[162]

They are all alleged victims of unscrupulous or incompetent advisors or business associate scammers posing as trusted financial advisors. Sadly, theft and other wrongdoings perpetrated against pro athletes also have an impact on the next generation. Not only did these people—who were in a position of trust and influence—rob these unsuspecting pro athletes of their future standard of living, but also the generational wealth that could have been stored for their children and their children's children.

Pro athletes are uniquely vulnerable to trusting the wrong people. A 2021 report by Ernst & Young estimated that, from 2004 through 2019, athletes across all sports alleged fraud-related losses of nearly $600M over the last 15 years.[163] Many believe the true amount is much higher, as a good deal of financial crimes are not reported. According to the report, fraud schemes against pro athletes vary but there is a common theme: The fraud perpetrator gains the athlete's trust, either directly or through mutual contacts, and leverages the relationship of trust into the fraudster's own financial windfall.

Defrauded athletes often do not report losses because many want to maintain their privacy, or because of the time it would take to follow through, or because they are too embarrassed to pursue litigation or don't bother because they assume the effort will be fruitless. Insurance claims may also play a role in their decision to pursue or not pursue the perpetrator(s).

In some cases, victims may not even be aware there have been improprieties. It is difficult to detect fraud. This is the major reason why it is imperative that the pro athlete thoroughly vet financial advisors and their firms and hire only reputable financial advisors. *An interesting tidbit:* When the transgressions against pro athletes hit the news, the "victims" do not receive the empathy they deserve. People think pro athletes make too much money anyway, and some even believe that they deserve to be exploited and think they should have known better. Are professional athletes actually victims? Or are their financial misfortunes the consequence of financial illiteracy?

Words to the wise:
Stop thieves in their track. If you see something, say something. If you have been a victim of fraud, the Commodity Futures Trading Commission (CFTC) created a list of six steps to take after discovering fraud. The link to the article is included in the Chapter Notes.[164]

Reason 43

Frontloaded/Backloaded

The R word. *Retirement* is universally recognized as a time of transition, but the R word may have a different meaning for you than your parents. For many pro athletes, the word *retirement* can have negative overtones. Regardless of how you feel about the R word, it's important—imperative—to plan for this eventual time of transition. It's the second act. What if you were encouraged at the very start of your professional career to begin with the end game in mind, financially? This is exactly what financial advisors ask clients to do. A common question we ask is "Where would you like to end up financially at the end of your sport's career?"

This is a hard question to ask a young athlete. Can you really put any focus on the end game when all your energy is going into becoming the best athlete, right now? You are training hard, getting paid well, and learning to enjoy the lifestyle you've worked so hard to attain. You are constantly asked to focus on a singular goal of winning—to be the best. Can adopting a mindset of planning for life after retirement detract you from being the best competitor in the here and now?

When you start your sports career, you hear from all the talking heads how short the career might be – truth is the average pro athlete will likely retire from his sport before he celebrates his 32nd birthday. Added to this narrative is the fact that there are so many things out of the athlete's control that could force him into an early retirement. With all of these unknowns, if the pro athlete does not put a financial plan in place *early* in his career, he risks not landing on solid financial footing once his sports career ends.

For non-athletes, retirement usually occurs after a long working career, where incomes are spread over a 25-year or 35-year period. Pro

228

athletes, by contrast, have only a few years to take advantage of their spectacular earning potential, then must transition into a period of "normal" income or perhaps no income for the rest of their income-producing lives. Many pro athletes earn in a single year or over a few years more than the average worker may earn in a lifetime. With this frontloaded income arrangement, pro athletes must stretch their high short-term earnings over a lifetime, saving a sufficient amount to supplement income from less lucrative second and third careers. The million-dollar question: *Will you be disciplined enough to spend less money now and live below your means when your income is high, so you can have a comfortable lifestyle on the back end?* Or will you have financial regrets after retiring from your sports career? It's a frontloaded/backloaded financial conundrum.

> *"There are two kinds of pains: regret and discipline. Regret weights tons and discipline weighs ounces."*
>
> —Jim Rohn, motivational speaker

Controlling your spending and living below your means are two of the major challenges on the front end of your sports career, but there are different challenges on the back end. Transitioning to retirement from a sports career is not just a career change, it's a complete lifestyle adjustment. At the end of elite competition, research shows that many pro athletes suffer a form of identity crisis—accompanied by a lot of emotions, mostly negative, as their entire lives are turned upside-down and inside-out. Added to the physical and mental stress of concluding a dopaminergic career, if the athlete did not plan his finances well, these combined stressors can spiral him into a deep depressive state.

This is why pro athletes at the top of their game need to start thinking about the R word; sooner in their career, rather than later. It is critically important to have a plan—or at least a flexible blueprint at the beginning of your professional career—to begin with the end in mind and stay vigilant to the hopeful prospect of long-term financial security.

NFL star Rob "Gronk" Gronkowski celebrated his first retirement at age 30 from the New England Patriots in 2019 after playing nine seasons, then came out of retirement to play his final two seasons with the Tampa Bay Buccaneers. In his book, *It's Good to be Gronk*, he wrote that he never touched "one dime of my signing bonus or NFL contract money,"[165] opting to live on the money he made from various endorsement deals he signed—which reportedly totaled nearly $3.5 million over his career up to that point. Gronk says watching some other athletes blow through their own multimillion-dollar contracts inspired him to always keep a sizable nest egg. "I just wanted to [save money] throughout my NFL career because I know that—and I've seen it with my own eyes—that it might not last long."[166] It is estimated that Gronkowski earned more than $60 million in his storybook 11-year NFL career. He may be an outlier, but conceptually his approach to frugal living, spending less, and saving for the future makes a lot of sense.

In August 2022, the GOAT and my favorite professional athlete, tennis legend Serena Williams, announced that at age 40 she was starting her transition away from tennis—being careful not to use the R word. She says, "I have never liked the word *retirement*. It doesn't feel like a modern word to me." She continues, "Maybe the best word to describe what I'm up to is evolution. I'm here to tell you that I'm evolving away from tennis, toward other things that are important to me."[167]

Photo Credit: flickr.com mirsasha

The GOAT: Serena Williams

Can we all agree that *retirement* is not the best word to use when discussing a pro athlete's decision to end one journey to start another? The world's perception of retirement is primarily age-based, typically people in their late 60s or early 70s and conjuring up a sight in the mind's eye of gray-haired individuals going off into the sunset—somber. When you look up the word *retirement* in a thesaurus, there are so many negative connotations: of being all washed up, finished, useless—like one has reached an expiration date of usefulness, non-relevance, no additional value that can be added to this world. Done.

But for pro athletes in their early to mid-30s, somehow the word *retirement* does not capture what these elite athletes are transitioning to for their next journey. "I've been reluctant to admit that I have to move on from playing tennis. It's like a taboo topic. It comes up, and I start to cry,"[168] Serena Williams shares about the R word. From a psychological perspective, this could be a reason why it is so difficult for pro athletes to begin with the end in mind. Who wants to think about the "end"?

Another factor complicating retirement planning for some pro athletes is that they divorce curiously soon after signing their largest guaranteed contract—having to forfeit half of their fortunes and ending up with sizable alimony and expensive child-support payments. Two high-profile alimony cases were recorded as the two most expensive divorce settlements in golf's history: Greg Norman reportedly paid his ex-wife $103 million,[169] and Tiger Woods reportedly paid his ex-wife $100 million.[170] And of course, there was NBA's hall of famer Michael Jordan's $168-million-dollar divorce.[171] Your income is frontloaded, but the bulk of your living expenses and financial challenges are backloaded.

There's good news. Most professional sport leagues now have retirement benefits including pension plans, 401(k) salary-deferral plans with matching funds, retiree medical health plans, and college-tuition-reimbursement programs, thanks to the hard-fought bargaining skills of the various CBA representatives.

Words to the wise:

Pro athletes should consider a three-tiered retirement plan:

1. Transition from an active sports career to a new second career,

2. Transition from the second career (or multiple second careers) to full retirement, and

3. Transition from retirement to eternity, which involves comprehensive estate/legacy planning.

Working with your vetted financial advisor(s), you should start with the end in mind—and with a focus on your future self:

- Save as much money as possible early in your career to take advantage of compound interest (see Reason #26). Plan for retirement by paying yourself first and living below your means.

- Implement tax-efficient strategies, including tax-free or tax-deferred savings, and a plan to relocate to a state that has favorable income tax laws. Be sure your plan is flexible. There's no need to rigidly commit to a strategy too early, as tax laws can and do change (see Reason #38). Make sure your tactical plan is sufficiently fluid.
- Know the qualifications of the league's/association's sponsored pension and healthcare plans, and max out the tax-deferred 401(k) retirement savings plan benefits. Also be aware of other benefits that are available to you and actively advocate for better, more desirable retirement benefits.
- Stay as healthy as possible (see Chapter 5).
- Stay out of debt, build wealth wisely, and invest in assets that appreciate (see Reason #8 and Reason #27).
- Keep estate-planning documents (power of attorney, will, trust, and beneficiary designations) current.

Once your written financial plan is complete (see Reason #20), tweak it on a regular basis, as things change, people change, laws change, and circumstances change.

> *"Financial freedom can only be achieved by a conscious choice. It's not an accident. It's not just merely by thinking, it's through grinding and doing what is necessary to get to that goal."*
>
> —David Angway

RECAP

43 Reasons Professional Athletes Go Broke

Chapter 1: Dealing with Family and Friends

1. They are notoriously loyal to their supporters/entourage.
2. They surround themselves with "yes" men, and they themselves are "yes" men."

3. *They allow fame to change who their "friends" are and are people-pleased.*

4. They fall prey to lifestyle creep.
5. They sign over their power of attorney to unqualified associates like their barber.
6. They choose non-credentialed friends and family members to be advisors.

Chapter 2: Dealing with Professionals and Your Money

7. They put too much trust in strangers.
8. They are allowed to receive an insane amount of cash advances and loans.
9. They allow their sports agent to do it all.
10. They do not thoroughly vet their financial advisor(s).
11. They neglect to ask three very important questions of their financial advisor(s).
12. They don't do thorough background checks on would-be business partners.
13. They don't get a second opinion on financial proposals.
14. They allow inexperienced tax preparers to be their tax advisors.
15. They sign important paperwork without understanding the fine print.

16. They don't ask questions about transactions on their bank/investment statements.
17. They don't adopt an alias, and they have no idea who has access to their personal data.
18. They are not advised to create and stick to a monthly spending plan (budget).
19. They are not advised about contingency planning and asking, "What if?"
20. They are not advised to create a forward-looking comprehensive financial plan.

Chapter 3: Dealing with Self and the Entrepreneurial Spirit

21. They don't invest in their brains.
22. They invest in poorly researched business ventures.
23. They are too generous and lend money to anyone who asks.
24. They lack emotional maturity and make poor financial decisions to try to compensate.
25. They don't trust their instincts and are pressured to make bad financial decisions.
26. **They have never heard of the Rule of 72 and don't understand compound interest.**
27. They don't understand how wealth is created.

Chapter 4: The Entourage, Entertainment, Consumptive Behaviors, and Dopamine

28. They spend too much money on their personal entourage.
29. They cave into the expectation to leave *big* tips.
30. They live large on the regular, spending mega bucks on bottle service.
31. They spend too much money and have trouble controlling dopaminergic urges.

Chapter 5: Mental and Physical Health

32. They believe they are invincible and will never get hurt.

33. They have many choices in which they can engage; they fear that they are missing out on opportunities that are better than the one they initial chose.
34. They suffer from imposter syndrome, possess insecurities, and lack self-esteem.
35. They set no moral boundaries, behave like mavericks, and gamble too much.
36. They make mental health an afterthought and don't hire a thought coach/sport psychologist.

Chapter 6: Dealing with the Law, Including Tax Law

37. They engage unknowingly and/or knowingly in illegal activities.
38. They don't understand the "jock tax," and how it impacts them and their future selves.
39. They choose the wrong state to live in.

Chapter 7: Groupies and Tinder Love

40. They father too many kids out of wedlock, therefore paying big bucks in child support in retirement.
41. They are divas, they marry divas who practice financial infidelity, and they do not draw up prenup agreements before marriage.

Chapter 8: Paradigm Shift

42. They are victims.
43. They don't think about life beyond sports, and they have no plans for the R word.

> *"Why is it far fetch[ed] for me to know finance when I have a business, pay taxes and own stocks? You gotta know about money to maintain it."*[172]
>
> —Cardi B on Twitter: @iamcardib

CONCLUSION

Let's keep this 100. We all have made some stupid decisions with our money. We all know someone who is spending too much or maybe living too large, in our assessment, pretending to be rich or richer than their perceived incomes would suggest. Everyone has an opinion about how others should live their lives and spend their money. The funny thing is none of these opinions are the same or similar—nor do they matter. The media is relentless with articles upon articles about professional athletes going broke, filing for bankruptcy, not paying child support, getting their homes foreclosed, having their cars repossessed, and about the poor state of their financial affairs.

Err'body throwing shade.

You've seen the ESPN Films 30 for 30: *Broke* documentary, yes? Does it really matter how professional athletes spend their money? Does it matter that an estimated 60% of pro athletes are in financial distress five years after retiring? Truth be told, it *is* perplexing and hard to comprehend how, after making such a large amount of money, anyone could end up broke and broken. Does the "dumb jock" stigma apply here? I don't believe this is the case. Success Coach Tony Robbins shares in his TED Talk "Why We Do What We Do"[173], that there are six basic needs all humans have and we will do whatever it takes to meet the top two needs that we value the most. It's a great TED Talk, I highly recommend you watch it. Many of us are hardwired to behave in a certain way to get our needs met. So what can be changed? A paradigm shift is needed. It's time to think differently about the value of money and start taking delayed gratification and saving for the future more seriously.

During their early playing days, pro athletes enjoy high income from league contracts, cash bonuses, and lucrative endorsement deals. Ascribing to YOLO and known for notoriously burning through their cash with reckless abandonment, many athletes admit they think the cash will keep flowing their way and will never end. This is a false premise.

Can you blame them? This mindset of invincibility is what made them successful in the first place. Pro athletes indulge in extravagant lifestyles and seemingly have an insatiable appetite for the best this world has to offer, unapologetically purchasing luxury cars, expansive homes, extravagant designer clothes, and flashy jewelry—aspirational stuff, and spending without restraint. Many of these young men are also generous to a fault, adding to their financial woes. Most pro athletes realize there is a stereotype of athletes being free spending, and many are cognizant of the mistakes made by other professional associates who played the spending game and went broke. Most don't want to make the same mistakes.

We live during a time when more information is generated now than at any time in history. Even with all the available information, many still lack the knowledge and wisdom to make sound financial decisions. Substantial changes in financial behaviors are needed to improve our money game. Financial literacy impacts the decisions you make every day—whether you're spending, saving, investing for a secure future, or starting a new business venture. Consequences of poor financial decisions are a major cause of personal stress and can lead to relationship issues in marriages or with a significant other as well as poor performance on the field, court, or track, which can exacerbate financial woes. Remember that *stop, drop, and roll* fire safety technique taught back in the day? I suggest a similar modus operandi of *pause, reflect, and investigate* when dealing with financial matters. Pause, and think through your options. Reflect, consider people you know or have heard about who were in a similar situation, and take mental notes about how they dealt with a similar financial issue. And investigate. Since you don't know what you don't know, you should get in the habit of asking a lot of questions about money issues.

In this book, I talked about the circumstances unique to your profession as a professional athlete that make financial planning more difficult than it is for other highly compensated professionals:

> ➤ Frontloaded income. You have shorter earning time spans than most other professions. You spend the first five to 12 years of

your economic life cycle—20% of your life —making money that must last 50+ years.

➤ Physiology of the brain/cognitive immaturity. You're young, and problem-solving skills do not fully develop in males until the age of about 27 or a few years thereafter.[174]

➤ Excessive dopamine. This can lead to compulsive and unrestrained spending.

➤ Unpredictable income streams. Due to contract uncertainties, injuries, and shorter-than-expected professional careers, your personal income can experience radical swings.

➤ Massive and hungry entourages.

➤ Lack of financial "know-how" and experience. Because of your inexperience and demanding schedule, you delegate your financial/business affairs to friends and advisors.

➤ Misplaced trust/unscrupulous advisors/unvetted business deals.

➤ Family matters (entitled family members, irremissible child support from unplanned fatherhood, and punishing alimony).

In addition to the above special circumstances, there are other reasons you may be susceptible to poor financial decision-making, including sociology, psychology, the speed at which you receive the money, making you an *instant* millionaire, the timing you receive the money while just entering adulthood, making you an *inexperienced* and *unlearned* millionaire, and the large amounts you receive over a short period of time, making you an *aspirational* millionaire with generational wealth potential. Contrary to the elite pro athlete narrative, the average age of millionaires is 59.[175]

Anecdotally, this means that it takes decades of hard work and sound money management to accumulate and maintain substantial wealth for the average millionaire to attain and maintain their status. Even many of today's multimillionaires have filed for bankruptcy a few times before getting the money game right. The seasoned veteran millionaire is afforded a mulligan or two (or three). This is generally not the case for young professional athletes who become insolvent after raking in millions during their playing days. There likely will not be a second chance for them. In doing the research for this book, it became clear to me that youth and inexperience may not be the ideal combination to make the best financial decisions. ***Without the ability to learn quickly,*** young elite athletes are at risk of not enjoying lifelong financial security after earning big cash during their professional sports careers.

A paradigm shift is needed in how you see and navigate your economic world. Poor money decisions caused by a lack of financial knowledge can result in a devastating hit to your financial well-being. Similar to the way you obsess about winning a championship, you should use an identical mindset to contemplate your financial future. Be mindful of your future self, love him like you love your current self, and take the necessary steps that will enable you to extend your current success into long-term financial independence. This intentionality will undoubtedly make your future self very proud. There are many success stories of professional athletes making the most of their financial opportunities: OG NBA Hall of Famer Michael Jordan, now majority stakeholder in the Charlotte Hornets, tennis great Serena Williams with Serena Ventures, NFL rockstar quarterbacks Peyton Manning and Tom Brady, who both have numerous profitable business ventures, boxing great George Foreman with the George Foreman Grill, WWE pro wrestler Dwayne "The Rock" Johnson, and NBA superstar LeBron James, co-founder of the Springhill Company.

It's rare for professional athletes to get a second chance to make real money after retiring from a sports career, but in 2019, Allen Iverson, who reportedly blew through more than $200 million of career earnings got his mulligan. Iverson signed a "second chance" lucrative opportunity in which he can cash in on a $32 million rainy-day trust fund sponsored by Reebok as part of a previous deal he made with the brand.[176] Although Iverson can't access the trust fund until 2030, this deferred compensation arrangement, dubbed *The Iverson Clause,* could be the answer (pun intended) to a future compensation template for professional athletes.

Instead of lump-sum payouts, would it be beneficial to have a compensation system that offers players the option of a series of payments over a longer period of time, providing a stable standard of living? Two authors of a National Bureau of Economic Research study, Annamaria Lusardi and Colin Camerer, suggest that there should be such a system so pro athletes can manage their earnings ebbs and flows to provide long-term financial stability.[177] Some players wisely set up their own income systems to manage their earning spike over the long term. Financial products that contractually deliver a guaranteed income for life with a residual refund might be a great financial product for pro athletes to ensure the receipt of income that lasts a lifetime.

The consequences of poor money decisions are long lasting, and the collateral damage can be widespread. It can take years to climb out of the financial abyss to get back on track. To get and stay on top of the money game, acknowledging a lack of financial know-how is the first step to improving financial literacy. Many young elite athletes just don't know what they don't know. An honest introspection is warranted. While admitting you need an open, unfiltered discussion on basic financial concepts and personal spending behaviors can be awkward, difficult, and downright intimidating, this self-awareness can lead you on a journey to getting the knowledge you need to make better decisions regarding your money. The sooner the financial knowledge improvement process starts, the better.

We all have a role to play to start making sound money moves. Pre-pandemic, only 14 states required students to take a personal finance course in high school to graduate.[178] After the economic shutdown caused by the pandemic, many more states are now introducing new financial literacy requirements for high school students. I recommend a protocol to have age-appropriate financial literacy curriculums in schools as early as second grade. Since no one is born knowing how to handle money, money-management skills must be taught. Parents must talk unapologetically to their kids about money and the family financial situation, especially the monthly budgeting dynamics.

> *"A study by Freddie Mac revealed that comprehension of the general principles of sound financial behavior, such as budgeting and savings, is actually more beneficial in producing successful financial results over time than specific and detailed information on financial transactions. These findings underscore the importance of **beginning the learning process as early as possible**. Indeed, in many respects, improving basic financial education at the elementary and secondary school level is essential to providing a foundation for financial literacy that can help prevent younger people from making poor financial decisions that can take years to overcome."[179]*
>
> —Alan Greenspan, former Chairman of the Federal Reserve (served 1987–2006)

The Financial Industry Regulatory Authority (FINRA) Foundation was established to help Americans build financial stability, invest for life goals, and guard against fraud by serving as a repository for data describing the financial capability of American households. The foundation sponsors the National Financial Capability Study, which examines the capability of Americans to make ends meet, plan personal finances, consume financial knowledge, and understand and manage financial products.[180]

It's encouraging to know financial institutions and other economic stakeholders are entering the financial education ecosystem. Netflix is ahead of the game with *Get Smart with Money,* a documentary that brings personal finance issues to the masses. Hasbro and Varsity Tutors teamed up to create Monopoly's Money Matters Financial Literacy Camp, a virtual, interactive adventure that teaches teenagers about budgeting, personal finance, marketing, entrepreneurship, and business strategy. More can and should be done. What if financial institutions partnered with social media influencers to engage their followers in real conversations on the topic of becoming more financially savvy? The financial advisory community could collaborate to create more age-specific interactive games and immersive virtual reality (VR) that make learning about financial decision-making more user-friendly and relevant. Wouldn't it be great if someone produced a reality TV program with real CFP® professionals and real people with real financial issues, highlighting real financial solutions? Employers could also play a role to increase financial literacy by offering more financial wellness workshops to their employees, making it a condition of employment. Yeah, it's that important.

The unspoken truth is young elite athletes rarely have teammates to model good financial decision-making behaviors. With so few good financial role models, poor financial decision-making is often passed on from sport generation to generation, season to season, and the cycle of financial illiteracy continues. What if the player associations and league ombudsmen took on a more active advocacy stance, maybe "assigning" a veteran as a financial mentor/sponsor to check in on rookies *and* their financial advisory team? Or at the very least, encouraging all rookies to listen to the audio-book *The Molecule of More* by Daniel Z. Lieberman, MD, and Michael E. Long and to use this book, *Making Sound Money Moves,* as a personal finance reference guide to making better decisions with their money. It's time to stop the insanity.

Financial literacy is important because it equips us with the knowledge and skills needed to make better decisions with our money. We must make a conscious effort not to sprint to the financial cliff but increase our intellectual capital and embrace sound money principles. Instead of placing a financial ambulance (bankruptcy) under the financial cliff awaiting the fall, we need to erect a financial literacy fence interwoven with behavior modifications on top of the cliff to stop the financial carnage. Make your future self proud by making better financial decisions today. In this age of massive information, financial illiteracy is a choice. It's time to *uplevel* your financial literacy game. Ready. Set. Grow!

> *"If people are constantly falling off a cliff, you could place ambulances under the cliff or build a fence on the top of the cliff. We are placing all too many ambulances under the cliff."*
>
> —Denis Parsons Burkitt

Question: After reading this book in its entirety, what would you do if you received $2 million dollars today?

_____

_____

_____

_____

_____

ACKNOWLEDGMENTS & INSPIRATION

To my sweetheart, ride or die, partner in life, Cliff Sr.—thank you for your love and support.

Thank you, Cliff Jr.—for the many discussions on what athletes might be thinking.

Thank you, Brandon—for listening to your mom and managing your money wisely.

Thank you, Darius—for encouraging me to finish this book: "Mom, Gen Zers don't read."

My Fam

Beta readers—you all ROCK!!! Thank you!

Sari, Vi, Cliff Sr., Cliff Jr., Brandon, LoRon, Holly and Rick, Adam (Brandon's Agent) and Cade — you are appreciated!

Cade Collenback, long snapper for the UTSA Roadrunners

Thank you John Wesley Lee III for my Steve Flowers *Missing You* jazz playlist.

Thank you to all my immediate and extended family, friends, and financial planning clients for your encouragement.

You are all appreciated!

~~~ INSPIRATION ~~~

Prue Road Hiking Trail in San Antonio, Texas, a beautiful hiking trail that helped me maintain clarity of vision during my daily 3.5-mile walks. I love, love this place.

"A Brand New Day," song performed on the album *The Wiz Live! (Original Soundtrack)*

"Believe For It (Eu Creio)," song by CeCe Winans and Gabriela Rocha

POSTSCRIPT 1

What Are Professional Sport Leagues and Player Associations Doing to Improve the Financial Literacy of Their Players?

Benefactors and Guardians of the Sports Industry:
Everyone Has a Role to Play – Each One, Teach One

Professional athletes around the world have multifaceted challenges with regard to managing their money, and many of the factors are not easily addressed. Financial literacy is a learned skill, and, while you spend a good amount of your time fine-tuning gifts and talents to improve your performance, your personal brand, and your team's success, time also must be allocated to learn how to make sound financial decisions so the desired financial security can be achieved after the playing days are over.

Owners, league leadership, and players' associations have important roles in the pro athlete support network ecosystem, second only to the fans who enjoy and enthusiastically patronize the sports. It's in everyone's best interest that those in the support ecosystem act as guardians of the sport they represent, and as such must place the well-being of their pro athlete members in the highest regard. Advocating for members to obtain proper financial information to become knowledgeable business partners makes sense for all parties involved. Empowerment is the name of the game. Here are a few of the things the professional sport community is doing to improve the financial literacy of their members. The list of programs available to date is respectable, but more can be done.

The following program information was summarized from the respective websites and are current at the time of the printing of this book.[181]

The NFL, in partnership with National Football League Players Association (NFLPA), has the National Football League Financial Education Program (NFL FEP), 4-Day Bootcamp for Players, which includes a financial education course. In April 2021, during Financial Literacy Month, the NFLPA launched a program called "Dropping Jewels" *to share jewels of financial knowledge to get every kid in America on the path to financial freedom.*

The organization recently started a podcast, #AthleteAnd, with the tagline *"You live to play. But it's not all you live for."*[182] According to the website, "#AthleteAnd was created to showcase the identity of NFL players off the field. [To] Meet financial literacy professors, CEOs, gamers, and entrepreneurs who tap into education and experiences that allow them to grow their passions outside the locker room."[183]

The NBA, in partnership with the National Basketball Players Association (NBPA), has an NBA Rookie Transition Program and NBPA Camps that include money-management courses.

The WNBA, in partnership with the Women's National Basketball Players Association (WNBPA), recently partnered with Arizona State University to offer eligible members and their dependents the opportunity to receive an undergraduate degree or enroll in financial education courses.

MLB, in partnership with the Major League Baseball Players Association (MLBPA), created a Rookie Career Development Program (RCDP), which includes courses in financial management.

The NHL, in partnership with the National Hockey League Players' Association (NHLPA), launched its Core Development Program in 2016 to help players further their education and assist with the transition to life after hockey.

MLS, in partnership with Major League Soccer Players Association (MLSPA), announced a program in 2019 to further their commitment to players' financial wellness with the expansion of their partnership with a provider of workplace financial wellness benefits.

Photo Credit: NBPA

Brandon with the NBPA Coaching Program

POSTSCRIPT 2

The Race Card

What Role Does Race Play in the Pro Athlete's Relationship with Money?[184]

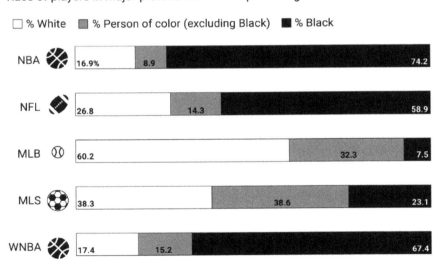

Racial diversity in US professional sports

Race of players in major professional team sports leagues*

☐ % White   ▨ % Person of color (excluding Black)   ■ % Black

NBA — 16.9% | 8.9 | 74.2

NFL — 26.8 | 14.3 | 58.9

MLB — 60.2 | 32.3 | 7.5

MLS — 38.3 | 38.6 | 23.1

WNBA — 17.4 | 15.2 | 67.4

Subscribe to our global politics newsletter Signal at gzeromedia.com

Source: University of Central Florida Institute for Diversity and Ethics in Sport
Notes: Data as of 2020 for NBA, as of 2019 for NFL, MLB, MLS and WNBA.
*The NHL does not release racial information about players.

GZERO

Let's start the conversation:

1. Is there unconscious racism in the money game? If so, who can level the playing field?
2. Does it matter that nearly 80% of the financial professionals who call themselves financial advisors are white[185]—with the majority being white males?
3. Why is fraud underreported by African-American pro athletes?

POSTSCRIPT 3

Money Moves Savvy Millennials (Gen Yers) and Gen Zers Should Make Right Now

No Wildin' Allowed

According to a Coldwell Banker report released in October 2019, there were 618,000 millennial millionaires in America with a net worth between $1M and $2.49M.[186] On the flip side, a different report by PYMNTS.com/Lending Club called Realty Check, published in June 2021, shows that more than 70% of millennials are living paycheck to paycheck.[187] Whichever side of the coin you're on, here are some sound money moves you can make today to improve your financial future:

- ✓ Create a vision for your financial future and set three major financial goals. Describe your vision in your mind's eye in vivid color and write it down. Share your vision and your goals with an accountability partner.

- ✓ Recruit an accountability partner (a trusted friend who is smart with money or a parent) to help you prioritize your financial goals. Getting your financial house in order can be hard work, and although you may be able to do this on your own, seeking help and support is important for this life-long journey. Sound money management is a marathon, not a sprint, and to the victor belong the spoils.

- ✓ Know your numbers. Based on the carefully curated vision for your financial future, determine how much money you need to make each year for the next five years—including thoughts about the amount you want to have accumulated in your savings account during that time. Do the exercise of pre-calculating your desired net worth (see Reason #27). Write

257

down your numbers and share them with your accountability partner.

✓ Prepare and stick to a monthly spending plan (see Reason #18). Examine your current spending habits and work toward the objective of not spending your entire paycheck. Spend less; save more.

✓ Overcome the present bias mindset and resist lifestyle creep (see Reason #4). Stop buying things that do not fit into *the vision* of your financial future. Eat out less, cook more, and hydrate with H2O between alcoholic beverages at bars.

✓ Pay off your debts and educate yourself about loans, credit cards, interest rates, and the folly of only making minimum payments (see Reason #8). Consider getting a side hustle (Uber, DoorDash, dog walking) to help pay off debts.

✓ Establish an emergency fund, saving enough to cover at least three months of expenses.

✓ Reread Reason #26. Make a commitment to understand compounding interest and maximize your 401(k) contributions. At the minimum, contribute the percentage to receive your employer's maximum match portion. Your future self will thank you.

POSTSCRIPT 4

Collegiate Athletes and the Name Image Likeness (NIL) NCAA Rule Change

A Special Note about Making Money Moves as a Student-Athlete

Effective July 1, 2021, the NCAA approved the NIL rule change, which allows all NCAA D1, D2, and D3 student-athletes to be compensated for their name, image, and likeness (NIL) rights. This means that student-athletes at colleges and universities across the country have, for the first time, the right to profit from their own name, their own image, and their own likeness. Once prohibited and penalized for having their own endorsement deals, student-athletes can now entertain sponsorships and influencer compensation deals due to a Supreme Court ruling that pushed the floodgates wide open. According to the NCAA, the policy provides the following guidance to college athletes, recruits, their families, and member schools regarding this new NIL opportunity:[188]

- Individuals can engage in NIL activities that are consistent with the laws of the state in which the school is located. Colleges and universities may be a resource to help student-athletes navigate state NIL laws.
- College athletes who attend a school in a state without an NIL law can engage in this type of activity authorized by the NCAA policy without violating NCAA rules related to name, image, and likeness.
- Student-athletes and their families can use a professional service to provide NIL guidance and activities.
- Student-athletes should report NIL activities consistent with state law or school and conference requirements of their school.

Many colleges and universities are taking an active role in trying to create specific opportunities by helping to organize endorsement deals to help student-athletes cash in on the new NIL rules and stay in compliance. For the student-athlete, money-making prowess and financial literacy challenges are top of mind. The time has come to understand and effectively use the money moves discussed in this book. As student-athletes across the country start to monetize their name, image, and likeness, sound financial decision-making will become more important than ever before. Hopefully this book inspires the student-athlete to do their homework and understand how to make sound money moves to improve chances at a financially successful future.

Student-athletes are getting sponsors and making the most of this new NIL rule change, be sure to optimize this opportunity. Check out these NIL money moves: nilcollegeathletes.com

Lynda in the hauzzzzz

Enhancing Financial Literacy Among Student-Athletes Report

Used with permission from the NCAA Financial Literacy, University of Texas and Kansas State University.

PROBLEM

Most college students, including student-athletes, have limited to no exposure to personal financial education when they arrive on campus. Without basic financial literacy, student-athletes, who are managing between different sources of income and how they use it, are at risk of increased stress and anxiety levels. Therefore, our goal was to identify both the level of financial literacy among student-athletes and the best way to reach them.

PILOT SOLUTION: MONEY 101 PROGRAM

- Free, non-credit 8-week course designed to introduce resources and tools that will help develop basic finance skills.
- 6 topics covered: money management, investing, credit, saving, paying for education, and working and earning.

CAMPUS-BASED APPLICATIONS

Buy-In from Student-Athletes

For a program like Money 101 to be successful, it is crucial to have buy-in from students. This can be achieved by hosting class once a week in-person, support from coaches, former student-athletes, and/or other role models, or personalizing content to student-athletes and their specific needs

Peer Financial Counseling

One-on-one financial counseling was the most preferred method for financial education. Peer financial counseling is desirable because of how students can relate to one another. In addition to the rigorous training peer financial counselors undergo, we suggest adding information regarding financial needs experienced by student-athletes. Financial counseling could be offered during required student hours or student athlete development sessions. If establishing a peer financial counseling center is not achievable, housing an alternative center under a related department such as Business Administration or Financial Planning could be an option.

Decreasing Spending

Almost half of the monthly transactions logged involved eating out. 24% of spending went to gas and fuel costs, which was second to housing costs. Athletic departments could host workshops that teach student-athletes how to cook affordable, nutritious meals and provide information on how they can save on purchases through rewards programs, rebates, and discounts.

KEY FINDINGS

SPENDING BEHAVIOR	INTEREST & EXPERIENCE	MONEY 101 & TEST RESULTS
• Of the 21% who had a monthly budget, 92% followed it • 47 % experience anxiety when managing money • When monthly spending was tracked, over 46% of transactions were food	• 7.26 was the average ranking when asked to identify their interest in financial literacy from a scale of 1 to 10 (1: not interested at all, 10: fully interested) • 60% did not receive financial education in high school • 65% did not receive financial education at college orientation	• Money 101 saw a 10% increase in score from the pre – to the post-test • When asked 3 financial knowledge questions on the pre-and post-test, 59.34% either answered all questions incorrectly on both or correct on one but incorrect on the other

2018 NCAA Innovations in Research and
Practice Grant Final Report.

Lisa M. Rubin, Kansas State University, Sonya Britt-Lutter, Kansas State University, Daron K. Roberts, The University of Texas at Austin, Arin C. Dunn, Kansas State University, Fanny Fang, Kansas State University, Camila Haselwood, Kansas State University, Taylor R. Brown, The University of Texas at Austin.

Visit my website to view or download the full PDF report.

LyndaPaul.com

CHAPTER NOTES

[1] Strachan, Maxwell. "Josh Childress Explains In Detail How Millionaire NBA Players Go Broke." HuffPost, April 17, 2015.
https://www.huffpost.com/entry/josh-childress-broke-millionaire-nba-players_n_7086392.

[2] "CJ McCollum Stands by Estimate of Players Living Paycheck to Paycheck." NBC Sports Northwest. NBC Sports, April 6, 2020.
https://www.nbcsports.com/northwest/portland-trail-blazers/cj-mccollum-stands-estimate-players-living-paycheck-paycheck.

[3] Superbowl Commercials. "Super Bowl LVI (56) Commercial: Crypto.com - The Moment of Truth (2022)." YouTube video, 0:30. February 17, 2022.
https://www.youtube.com/watch?v=s0bRKbbGwtA.

[4] President's Advisory Council on Financial Literacy. "2008 Annual Report to the President." Scribd. Public Archive, January 16, 2009.
https://www.scribd.com/document/135313221/Pacfl-Annual-Report-1-16-09.

[5] "Financial Illiteracy Cost Americans $1,819 in 2022." National Financial Educators Council, January 12, 2023.
https://www.financialeducatorscouncil.org/financial-illiteracy-costs-2

[6] Johnson, Eddie A. *You Big Dummy - An Athlete's "SIMPLE" Guide To A Successful Career*. Independently Published, 2013.

[7] McCormick, Douglas P. "Financial Literacy--The Big Problem No One Is Talking About." HuffPost, June 3, 2017.
https://www.huffpost.com/entry/financial-literacythe-big_b_10264622/amp.

[8] Gough, Christina. "North America Sports Market Size from 2009 to 2023 (in Billion U.S. Dollars)*." Statista, July 27, 2022.
https://www.statista.com/statistics/214960/revenue-of-the-north-american-sports-market/.

[9] Ultimate Texans. "Warren Sapp on Jadeveon Clowney: 'You're Disappointing Us.'" Chron. The Houston Chronicle, November 3, 2014.
https://blog.chron.com/ultimatetexans/2014/11/warren-sapp-on-jadeveon-clowney-youre-disappointing-us/.

[10] ""Stephen Curry Contract, Salary Cap Details & Breakdowns." Spotrac, August 6, 2021.
https://www.spotrac.com/nba/golden-state-warriors/stephen-curry-6287/.

[11] Gough, Christina. "North America Sports Market Size from 2009 to 2023 (in Billion U.S. Dollars)*." Statista, July 27, 2022.
https://www.statista.com/statistics/214960/revenue-of-the-north-american-sports-market/.

[12] Busbee, Jay. "Phil Mickelson Warns of 'Drastic Changes' Because of State, Federal Tax Situation [UPDATED]." Yahoo!Sports. Yahoo!, January 21, 2013. https://sports.yahoo.com/blogs/golf-devil-ball-golf/phil-mickelson-warns-drastic-changes-because-state-federal-165909894--golf.html?guccounter=1.

[13] "Arthur J. Rooney in 1983." pittsburghsteelers.co.uk. Accessed March 31, 2023. http://www.pittsburghsteelers.co.uk/steelers/rooneys/page4.htm.

[14] Butowsky, Ed. "How and Why Professional Athletes Go Broke - Ed Butowski." YouTube video, 34:36. December 7, 2012. https://www.youtube.com/watch?v=hqJqqbpcc4E.

[15] Torre, Pablo S. "How (and Why) Athletes Go Broke." Vault. Sports Illustrated, March 23, 2009. https://vault.si.com/vault/2009/03/23/how-and-why-athletes-go-broke.

[16] Admin. "What Is the Average Age Athletes Retire?" Sage-Answer, July 5, 2019. https://sage-answer.com/what-is-the-average-age-athletes-retire/.

[17] "At What Age Is the Brain Fully Developed?" Mental Health Daily, February 18, 2015. https://mentalhealthdaily.com/2015/02/18/at-what-age-is-the-brain-fully-developed/.

[18] Torre, Pablo S. "How (and Why) Athletes Go Broke." Vault. Sports Illustrated, March 23, 2009. https://vault.si.com/vault/2009/03/23/how-and-why-athletes-go-broke.

[19] Torre, Pablo S. "How (and Why) Athletes Go Broke." Vault. Sports Illustrated, March 23, 2009. https://vault.si.com/vault/2009/03/23/how-and-why-athletes-go-broke.

[20] Anonymous. Quoted by Fred Rose Rotary Club-Central Senior class meeting. Date unknown.

[21] "Average IQ of Professional Athletes [Best Guide]." Personality Tests Center, February 11, 2021. https://personalityanalysistest.com/average-iq/average-iq-of-professional-athletes-best-guide/.

[22] Averill, Erik. "Athlete CEO #035: Advice All Pro Athletes Need | Zach Miller." *Athlete CEO,* September 17, 2020. Podcast, website, 29:02. https://awmcap.com/podcast/athlete-ceo-035-miller.

[23] National Center for Education Statistics. "National Assessment of Adult Literacy (NAAL): A First Look at the Literacy of America's Adults in the 21st Century." Washington, D.C.: U.S. Department of Education, 2003. https://nces.ed.gov/NAAL/PDF/2006470.PDF.

[24] Roth, J.D. "Why Financial Literacy Fails (and What to Do about It)." Get Rich Slowly, April 24, 2019. https://www.getrichslowly.org/why-financial-literacy-fails-and-what-to-do-about-it/.

[25] Klontz, Brad, Sonya L. Britt, and Ted Klontz. "Money Beliefs and Financial Behaviors: Development of the Klontz Money Script Inventory." *The Journal of Financial Therapy* 2, no. 1 (2011). https://doi.org/10.4148/jft.v2i1.451.

26 Klontz, Brad, Sonya L. Britt, and Ted Klontz. "Money Beliefs and Financial Behaviors: Development of the Klontz Money Script Inventory." *The Journal of Financial Therapy* 2, no. 1 (2011). https://doi.org/10.4148/jft.v2i1.451.

27 Wilson, Timothy D. *Strangers to Ourselves: Discovering the Adaptive Unconscious.* Cambridge, MA: Belknap Press of Harvard University Press, 2002.

28 Arnott, Sherwin. "The GI Joe Fallacy: Knowing Is Not Half the Battle: Interrobang Magazine." Emotional Intelligence Field Notes. The Emotional Intelligence Training Company, May 16, 2016. https://www.emotionalintelligence.ca/2016/05/the-gi-joe-fallacy-knowing-is-not-half-the-battle-interrobang-magazine/.

29 Associated Press. "Ohio State vs. Illinois - Men's College Basketball Game Recap - January 10, 2012." ESPN, January 11, 2012. https://www.espn.com/mens-college-basketball/recap/_/gameId/320100356.

30 "Samuel Smiles Quotes." BrainyQuote.com, BrainyMedia Inc, 2023. https://www.brainyquote.com/quotes/samuel_smiles_163293.

31 "The Importance of Teen Friendships." Newport Academy, June 13, 2022. https://www.newportacademy.com/resources/empowering-teens/teen-friendships/.

32 Paul, Lynda. *Making Sound Money Moves: Financial Playbook for All Jocks - 43 Reasons Professional Athletes Have Jacked-Up Financial Lives and What You Can Learn from Their Foul Plays.* Salt Lake City, UT: Elite Online Publishing, 2023.

33 Petkac, Luke. "The Anatomy of an NBA Entourage." Bleacher Report, March 8, 2013. https://bleacherreport.com/articles/1558549-the-anatomy-of-an-nba-entourage.

34 Bucher, Ric. "If You Don't Love It, Why Do It?': How Klay Thompson's Family Made Him a Star." Bleacher Report, May 8, 2018. https://bleacherreport.com/articles/2774734-klay-thompson-may-not-act-like-a-superstar-but-he-sure-as-hell-is.

35 Petkac, Luke. "The Anatomy of an NBA Entourage." Bleacher Report, March 8, 2013. https://bleacherreport.com/articles/1558549-the-anatomy-of-an-nba-entourage.

36 Florio, Mike. "Deion Thinks Millionaire Athletes Need to Hire a 'No Man.'" ProFootballTalk. NBC Sports, July 12, 2011. https://profootballtalk.nbcsports.com/2011/07/12/deion-thinks-millionaire-athletes-need-to-hire-a-no-man/.

37 Farlex International. *The Farlex Idioms and Slang Dictionary.* Independently Published, 2017.

38 Strachan, Maxwell. "Josh Childress Explains In Detail How Millionaire NBA Players Go Broke." HuffPost, April 17, 2015. https://www.huffpost.com/entry/josh-childress-broke-millionaire-nba-players_n_7086392.

39 Housel, Morgan. *The Psychology of Money: Timeless Lessons on Wealth, Greed, and Happiness.* Petersfield, UK: Harriman House, 2020.

40 Cohn, Scott. "This Financial Document—in the Wrong Hands—Burned Some Sports Legends. You Could Be at Risk, Too." CNBC, February 28, 2020.

https://www.cnbc.com/2020/02/28/this-financial-documentin-the-wrong-handsburned-some-sports-legends.html.
[41] Pavone, Barbara. "The Truth About Peggy Fulford's Multi-Million Dollar Scam With The Biggest Sports Stars In The World." Nicki Swift, December 3, 2021. https://www.nickiswift.com/668680/the-truth-about-peggy-fulfords-multi-million-dollar-scam-with-the-biggest-sports-stars-in-the-world/.
[42] "Becoming an Agent." NFL Players Association. Accessed April 1, 2023. https://nflpa.com/agents/how-to-become-an-agent.
[43] "NBPA Certified Agents." National Basketball Players Association. Accessed April 1, 2023. https://nbpa.com/agents/.
[44] "MLBPA Agent Certification." Major League Baseball Players Association. Accessed April 1, 2023. https://registration.mlbpa.org/Landing.aspx.
[45] "The Certification Process." CFP Board. Accessed April 1, 2023. https://www.cfp.net/get-certified/certification-process.
[46] "Learn What It Takes to Become a CPA." AICPA & CIMA, January 31, 2021. https://www.aicpa-cima.com/resources/download/learn-what-it-takes-to-become-a-cpa.
[47] Gladwell, Malcolm. *Talking to Strangers: What We Should Know about the People We Don't Know.* 1st ed. New York, NY: Little, Brown and Company, 2019.
[48] Gladwell, Malcolm. *Talking to Strangers: What We Should Know about the People We Don't Know.* 1st ed. New York, NY: Little, Brown and Company, 2019.
[49] Levine, Timothy R. "Truth-Default Theory (TDT)." Timothy R. Levine. Accessed April 1, 2023. https://timothy-levine.squarespace.com/truth-default-theory.
[50] Bensinger, Graham. "How Shaq spent $1 Million in one day." YouTube video, 04:13. November 20, 2015. https://www.youtube.com/watch?v=wMpZgt6agpU.
[51] Hurd, Erin, and Lindsay Konsko. "Credit Cards Can Make You Spend More, but It's Not the Full Story." NerdWallet, October 14, 2022. https://www.nerdwallet.com/article/credit-cards/credit-cards-make-you-spend-more.
[52] "Personal Financial Advisors." Occupational Outlook Handbook. U.S. Bureau of Labor Statistics, September 8, 2022. https://www.bls.gov/ooh/business-and-financial/personal-financial-advisors.htm.
[53] Kim, Hugh H., Raimond Maurer, and Olivia S. Mitchell. "How Financial Literacy Shapes the Demand for Financial Advice at Older Ages." *The Journal of the Economics of Ageing* 20 (October 2021). https://doi.org/10.1016/j.jeoa.2021.100329.
[54] Katzeff, Paul. "How Financial Advisors Should Deal With The 32% Of Americans Who Mistrust Them." Investor's Business Daily, June 1, 2017. https://www.investors.com/financial-advisors/how-financial-advisors-should-deal-with-the-32-of-americans-who-mistrust-them/.
[55] "What Is a Fiduciary?" Consumer Financial Protection Bureau, August 5, 2016. https://www.consumerfinance.gov/ask-cfpb/what-is-a-fiduciary-en-1769/.

56 "Quote by Lou Holtz: 'The Man Who Complains about the Way the Ball Bounces Is Likely the One Who Dropped It.'" Goodreads. Accessed April 1, 2023. https://www.goodreads.com/quotes/267197-the-man-who-complains-about-the-way-the-ball-bounces.
57 Deane, Michael T. "Top 6 Reasons New Businesses Fail." Edited by Khadija Khartit and Katharine Beer. Investopedia, December 30, 2022. https://www.investopedia.com/financial-edge/1010/top-6-reasons-new-businesses-fail.aspx.
58 Bensinger, Graham. "How Shaq spent $1 Million in one day." YouTube video, 04:13. November 20, 2015. https://www.youtube.com/watch?v=wMpZgt6agpU.
59 Martin, Emmie. "NBA Star Chris Bosh: I Have Millions and Know Nothing about Money." Yahoo!Finance. Yahoo!, March 9, 2018. https://finance.yahoo.com/news/nba-star-chris-bosh-millions-141800635.html.
60 Malone, George. "7 NFL Players Who Have Negotiated Their Own Contracts—How They Did." Yahoo Finance, January 18, 2021. https://finance.yahoo.com/news/7-nfl-players-negotiated-own-170054001.html.
61 Burnett, Jane. "Survey: 36% of Americans Look at Their Bank Account Daily." TheLadders, August 17, 2018. https://www.theladders.com/career-advice/survey-36-of-americans-look-at-their-bank-account-daily.
62 PYMNTS. Reality Check: The Paycheck-to-Paycheck Report December 2021. San Francisco, CA: LendingClub, 2021. https://www.pymnts.com/study/reality-check-paycheck-to-paycheck-pandemic-inflation-rising-costs/.
63 "2023 Identity Theft Facts and Statistics." IdentityTheft.org, 2023. https://identitytheft.org/statistics/.
64 "2023 Identity Theft Facts and Statistics." IdentityTheft.org, 2023. https://identitytheft.org/statistics/.
65 "FICO® Scores Are Used by 90% of Top Lenders." FICO® Score. Accessed April 1, 2023. https://www.ficoscore.com/about.
66 "CJ McCollum Stands by Estimate of Players Living Paycheck to Paycheck." NBC Sports Northwest. NBC Sports, April 6, 2020. https://www.nbcsports.com/northwest/portland-trail-blazers/cj-mccollum-stands-estimate-players-living-paycheck-paycheck.
67 "CJ McCollum Stands by Estimate of Players Living Paycheck to Paycheck." NBC Sports Northwest. NBC Sports, April 6, 2020. https://www.nbcsports.com/northwest/portland-trail-blazers/cj-mccollum-stands-estimate-players-living-paycheck-paycheck.
68 Clason, George S. The Richest Man in Babylon. New York, NY: Penguin Books, 1926.
69 White, Alexandria. "61% Of Americans Will Run out of Emergency Savings by the End of the Year—Here's How to Reduce Expenses Now." CNBC Select. CNBC, March 16, 2023.

https://www.cnbc.com/select/americans-running-out-of-emergency-savings-in-2020/.

[70] Carney, Logan. "Dwayne Haskins Signs One-Year RFA Tender with Steelers." SteelersNow, March 16, 2022.
https://steelersnow.com/dwayne-haskins-signs-one-year-rfa-tender/.

[71] "Brain Anatomy and How the Brain Works | Johns Hopkins Medicine." Johns Hopkins Medicine. The Johns Hopkins University, The Johns Hopkins Hospital, and Johns Hopkins Health System. Accessed April 1, 2023.

[72] Chernev, Bobby. "What Percentage of Startups Fail? [30+ Stats for 2023]." Review42, March 17, 2023.
https://review42.com/resources/what-percentage-of-startups-fail.

[73] Silvia. "5 Reasons Why Giving Makes You Happy (Based on Studies)." Tracking Happiness, January 29, 2023.
https://www.trackinghappiness.com/why-giving-makes-you-happy.

[74] Hanson, Dana. "The 20 Most Charitable Athletes in the World." Money Inc, March 27, 2023.
https://moneyinc.com/most-charitable-athletes-in-the-world/.

[75] "Emotional Maturity." APA Dictionary of Psychology. American Psychological Association. Accessed April 1, 2023.
https://dictionary.apa.org/emotional-maturity.

[76] Brennan, Dan. "What Is Emotional Immaturity." WebMD, October 25, 2021.
https://www.webmd.com/mental-health/what-is-a-emotional-immaturity.

[77] Lisa, Andrew. "24 Athletes Who Lost Their Huge Endorsement Deals." Yahoo!Finance. Yahoo!, August 14, 2019.
https://finance.yahoo.com/news/24-athletes-lost-huge-endorsement-090239873.html.

[78] "5 Ways to Get Better at Trusting Your Gut." RALI, July 13, 2020.
https://ralionline.com/newsinsights/5-ways-to-get-better-at-trusting-your-gut/.

[79] Paul, Lynda. *Making Sound Money Moves: Financial Playbook for All Jocks - 43 Reasons Professional Athletes Have Jacked-Up Financial Lives and What You Can Learn from Their Foul Plays*. Salt Lake City, UT: Elite Online Publishing, 2023.

[80] Nordstrom, Johan. "Step by Step Strategies and Signals That Work - Trading Walk." Trading Walk. Accessed April 1, 2023.
https://tradingwalk.com/start.

[81] Davis,Scott. "Manny Pacquiao Spent $3 Million on Fight Tickets for His Legendary Entourage." Business Insider, April 30, 2015.
https://www.businessinsider.com/manny-pacquiao-fight-tickets-entourage-2015-4.

[82] ClutchPoint. "How Allen Iverson Blew Through $200 Million, but Was Saved by a Secret Clause." Clutch Point, September 10, 2021.
https://clutchpoints.com/how-allen-iverson-blew-through-200-million-but-was-saved-by-a-secret-clause?amp=1.

[83] Petkac, Luke. "The Anatomy of an NBA Entourage." Bleacher Report, March 8, 2013. https://syndication.bleacherreport.com/amp/1558549-the-anatomy-of-an-nba-entourage.amp.html.

84 VLADTV "Andre Rison on Being on ESPN's 30 for 30 'Broke', Had 40 Person Entourage, Gave Away $6M (Part 16)." YouTube Video, September 18, 2020. https://youtu.be/uDvB4NSGnyA.

85 Lamare, Amy. "$400k on Pigeons and Tigers—That's Just One of The Splurges that Punched Out Mike Tyson's Peak $300 Million Fortune." Celebrity Net Worth, April 21, 2002 https://www.celebritynetworth.com/articles/entertainment-articles/how-did-mike-tyson-manage-to-blow-through-400-million.

86 Bednall, Jai. "Floyd Mayweather Has a Man for Everything." Fox Sports, November 10, 2022. https://www.foxsports.com.au/more-sports/floyd-mayweather-has-a-man-for-everything/news-story/e8bb6578aa2a174b066be154d667ab51.

87 Lee, Amber. "25 Insane Athlete Purchases." Bleacher Report, January 4, 2013. https://bleacherreport.com/articles/1467706-25-insane-athlete-purchases.

88 Lieberman, Daniel Z., and Michael E. Long. *The Molecule of More: How a Single Chemical in Your Brain Drives Love, Sex, and Creativity—and Will Determine the Fate of the Human Race.* Dallas, TX: BenBella Books, Inc., 2018.

89 "Why Retail 'Therapy' Makes You Feel Happier." HealthEssentials. Cleveland Clinic, January 21, 2021. https://health.clevelandclinic.org/retail-therapy-shopping-compulsion/.

90 "Why Retail 'Therapy' Makes You Feel Happier." HealthEssentials. Cleveland Clinic, January 21, 2021. https://health.clevelandclinic.org/retail-therapy-shopping-compulsion/.

91 "Why Retail 'Therapy' Makes You Feel Happier." HealthEssentials. Cleveland Clinic, January 21, 2021. https://health.clevelandclinic.org/retail-therapy-shopping-compulsion/.

92 Lieberman, Daniel Z., and Michael E. Long. *The Molecule of More: How a Single Chemical in Your Brain Drives Love, Sex, and Creativity—and Will Determine the Fate of the Human Race.* Dallas, TX: BenBella Books, Inc., 2018.

93 Etienne, Vanessa. "Russell Wilson Says He Spends $1 Million a Year on His Body, Hopes to Play in NFL until He's 45." People, March 2, 2022. https://people.com/sports/russell-wilson-spends-one-million-a-year-on-his-body-to-play-in-nfl/.

94 Etienne, Vanessa. "Russell Wilson Says He Spends $1 Million a Year on His Body, Hopes to Play in NFL until He's 45." People, March 2, 2022. https://people.com/sports/russell-wilson-spends-one-million-a-year-on-his-body-to-play-in-nfl/.

95 Wardleigh, Chakell. "Swimmer Michael Phelps Contemplated Suicide but Was Rescued by His Faith in God." Times-Mail, September 21, 2016. https://www.tmnews.com/story/lifestyle/faith/2016/09/21/swimmer-michael-phelps-contemplated-suicide-but-was-rescued-by-his-faith-in-god/48782523/.

96 Aldrin, Buzz, and Ken Abraham. *Magnificent Desolation: The Long Journey Home from the Moon.* London, UK: Bloomsbury Publishing , 2009.

97 Aldrin, Buzz, and Ken Abraham. *Magnificent Desolation: The Long Journey Home from the Moon.* London, UK: Bloomsbury Publishing , 2009.

98 Perkins-Gough, Deborah. "The Significance of Grit: A Conversation with Angela Lee Duckworth." Association for Supervision and Curriculum Development, September 1, 2013. https://www.ascd.org/el/articles/the-significance-of-grit-a-conversation-with-angela-lee-duckworth.

99 "The Shamrock System – Plus, Minus, and Equal." Leadership Freak, March 18, 2019. https://leadershipfreak.blog/2019/03/18/the-shamrock-system-plus-minus-and-equal/.

100 "In 2005, the National Science Foundation Published an Article Showing That the Average Person Has between 12,000 and 60,000 Thoughts per Day. Of Those, 80% Are Negative and 95% Are Exactly the Same Repetitive Thoughts as the Day before." Notes VTH. Accessed April 1, 2023. https://notes.vth.me/in-2005-the-national-science-foundation-published-an-article-showing-that-the-average-person-has-between-12000-and-60000-thoughts-per-day-of-those-80-are-negative-and-95-are-exactly-the-same-repe/.

101 Kross, Ethan. Chatter: The Voice in Our Head, Why It Matters, and How to Harness It. New York, NY: Crown, 2021.

102 TEDx Talks. "Imposter Syndrome By Any Other Name, Is Bravery | Catherine Harmon Toomer MD | TEDxCariobaStudio." YouTube video, 10:53. September 1, 2021. https://www.youtube.com/watch?v=SeLmwYdegLA.

103 "Lance Armstrong: I'd Have Won The Tour De France If Everyone Was Clean." Cycling News, July 10, 2019. https://www.cyclingnews.com/news/lance-armstrong-id-have-won-the-tour-de-france-if-everyone-was-clean/.

104 Vera, Amir, and David Close. "Jeff Gladney, Arizona Cardinals Cornerback, Dies at 25." CNN, May 31, 2022. https://www.cnn.com/2022/05/30/us/jeff-gladney-nfl-arizona-cardinals-death/index.html.

105 Bensinger, Graham. "John Daly: I lost $55 million gambling." YouTube video, 04:32. June 29, 2016. https://www.youtube.com/watch?v=PW8gDTY2b68.

106 Bensinger, Graham. "John Daly: I lost $55 million gambling." YouTube video, 04:32. June 29, 2016. https://www.youtube.com/watch?v=PW8gDTY2b68.

107 VLADTV. "Michael Franzese on Charles Barkley Losing $10M Gambling, He's the Addict Not Jordan (Part 4)." YouTube video, 08:10. June 19, 2020. https://www.youtube.com/watch?v=uDvB4NSGnyA.

108 Bensinger, Graham. "Charles Barkley on gambling: Lost $1 million 10-20 times." YouTube video, 02.57. April 27, 2016. https://www.youtube.com/watch?v=HJVdk6FlO24.

109 Harig, Bob. "Exclusive: Phil Mickelson On LIV Golf and His PGA Tour Status, 'I Have Not Resigned My Membership'." Sports Illustrated, June 6, 2022. https://www.si.com/golf/news/exclusive-phil-mickelson-on-liv-golf-and-his-pga-tour-status.

110 Augustus, Luke. "Michael Jordan Becomes First-Ever Billion Dollar Athlete as Forbes Ranks NBA Legend as 1741st Richest Person in the World." MailOnline. Daily Mail, March 3, 2015. https://www.dailymail.co.uk/sport/othersports/article-2977757/Michael-Jordan-billion-dollar-athlete-Forbes-ranks-NBA-legend-1741st-richest-man-world.html.

111 Hehir, Jason, dir. *The Last Dance*, Season 1, Episode 1, "Episode I." Aired April 19, 2020 on Netflix.

112 Retro Basketball Highlights. "Michael Jordan/Ahmad Rashād Interview 1993 Finals Game 1." YouTube video, 06:16. June 30, 2014. https://www.youtube.com/watch?v=1iXHS5Ri73g.

113 Wang, Lydia. "Simone Biles: 'We're Not Just Entertainment, We're Humans.'" Refinery29, August 3, 2021. https://www.refinery29.com/en-us/2021/08/10611521/simone-biles-statement-mental-health-olympics.

114 Lieberman, Daniel Z., and Michael E. Long. *The Molecule of More: How a Single Chemical in Your Brain Drives Love, Sex, and Creativity—and Will Determine the Fate of the Human Race*. Dallas, TX: BenBella Books, Inc., 2018.

115 "Sports Psychology Information Guide." All-About-Psychology.com. Accessed April 2, 2023. https://www.all-about-psychology.com/sports-psychology.html.

116 Meister, Alyson, and Maude Lavanchy. "Athletes Are Shifting the Narrative around Mental Health at Work." Harvard Business Review, September 24, 2021. https://hbr.org/2021/09/athletes-are-shifting-the-narrative-around-mental-health-at-work.

117 ESPN. "Kevin Love opens up in exclusive interview about mental health issues in the NBA [FULL] | ESPN." YouTube video, 45:11. August 24, 2018. https://www.youtube.com/watch?v=sW2LVIp9QcU.

118 ESPN. "Kevin Love opens up in exclusive interview about mental health issues in the NBA [FULL] | ESPN." YouTube video, 45:11. August 24, 2018. https://www.youtube.com/watch?v=sW2LVIp9QcU.

119 Rogers Behavioral Health. "A discussion on mental health with NFL's Solomon Thomas." YouTube video, 57:34. November 2, 2021. https://www.youtube.com/watch?v=Hv2bPlQhZvc

120 "Mental Health and Wellness Department." National Basketball Players Association. Accessed April 3, 2023. https://nbpa.com/mentalwellness.

121 "100+ Les Brown Quotes for Success in Life." Elijah Notes, February 6, 2020. https://www.elijahnotes.com/les-brown-quotes/.

122 Haislop, Tadd. "Aaron Hernandez Timeline: From Murders and Trials to Prison Suicide." The Sporting News, January 18, 2020. https://www.sportingnews.com/us/nfl/news/aaron-hernandez-timeline-murders-trials-prison-suicide/1886y82a8bgyx123qxcgg04lb5.

123 Page, Maxine. "What Michael Vick's Life in Prison Was Really Like." MSN. Microsoft Start, September 28, 2022. https://www.msn.com/en-us/sports/nfl/what-michael-vicks-life-in-prison-was-really-like/ar-AA12mmqT.

124 Chetia, Aklanta. "Legendary Swimmer Michael Phelps Lost Deal with a Billion-Dollar Company after His Infamous Act." EssentiallySports, May 26, 2022. https://www.essentiallysports.com/us-sports-news-swimming-news-legendary-swimmer-michael-phelps-lost-deal-with-a-billion-dollar-company-after-his-infamous-act/.
125 Katersky, Aaron. "18 Former NBA Players Charged with Defrauding the NBA's Health and Welfare Benefit Plan." ABC News, October 7, 2021. https://abcnews.go.com/amp/US/18-nba-players-charged-defrauding-nbas-health-welfare/story?id=80456611.
126 Murphy, Patrick. "THE DATABASE OF NFL ARREST STATISTICS." NFL Arrest. Accessed April 2, 2023. https://www.nflarrest.com/.
127 Bronars, Stephen, and Adam Ozimek. "The NFL's Violent Crime Problem." Forbes, April 29, 2015. https://www.forbes.com/sites/modeledbehavior/2015/04/29/the-nfls-violent-crime-problem/?sh=331dbdae1b95.
128 Lemoncelli, Jenna. "Henry Ruggs Was Driving 156 Mph, Had Double Legal BAC before Deadly Crash: Prosecutor." New York Post, November 3, 2021. https://nypost.com/2021/11/03/henry-ruggs-was-driving-156-mph-before-deadly-crash-prosecutor/.
129 Feldman, Dan. "Stephen Curry Signing Four-Year, $215M Contract Extension with Warriors." NBC Sports, August 2, 2021. https://nba.nbcsports.com/2021/08/02/report-stephen-curry-signing-four-year-215m-contract-extension-with-warriors/.
130 Wood, Robert W. "Tiger Woods Moved Too, Says Mickelson Was Right about Taxes." Forbes, January 23, 2013. https://www.forbes.com/sites/robertwood/2013/01/23/tiger-woods-moved-too-says-mickelson-was-right-about-taxes/?sh=777866e12b60.
131 AWM Capital. "The Tax Planning Strategy That Many NFL Players Miss | NFL Players' Podcast | Zach Miller." YouTube video, 07:13. December 30, 2020. https://www.youtube.com/watch?v=NfXsWzvP8cY.
132 Badenhausen, Kurt. "Full List: The World's Highest-Paid Athletes 2017." Forbes, June 15, 2017. https://www.forbes.com/sites/kurtbadenhausen/2017/06/15/full-list-the-worlds-highest-paid-athletes-2017/?sh=33c340cd583b.
133 Walczak, Jared. "Pittsburgh Claims Home-Field Advantage, but Visiting Athletes Cry Foul." Tax Foundation, November 8, 2019. https://taxfoundation.org/pittsburgh-jock-tax/.
134 Bilton, Nick. "Tinder, the Fast-Growing Dating App, Taps an Age-Old Truth." The New York Times, October 29, 2014. https://www.nytimes.com/2014/10/30/fashion/tinder-the-fast-growing-dating-app-taps-an-age-old-truth.html?_r=1.
135 "Tinder Saw 3 Billion Swipes within One Time as Social Distancing Increases." PryntControl, August 20, 2022.
136 RestlessRick. "Dennis Rodman's night out to show how some women chase NBA players (1996)." YouTube video, 02:19. May 1, 2020.

https://www.youtube.com/watch?v=FTp4Tfa-0-k.

137 "Divorce and Family Law Issues for Professional Athletes." Justia, July 2022. https://www.justia.com/sports-law/divorce-and-family-law-issues-for-professional-athletes/.

138 "Homepage." CarlaShow.com. Accessed April 2, 2023. https://carlashow.com/.

139 Sarkar, Raj. "Evander Holyfield's Kids: Who Are They, and What Are They Doing?" EssentiallySports, September 7, 2021. https://www.essentiallysports.com/boxing-news-evander-holyfields-kids-who-are-they-and-what-are-they-doing/.

140 Ifeoluwa, Damilola. "Who Are NBA Star Dwight Howard's Children?" TheThings, November 11, 2021. https://www.thethings.com/who-nba-star-dwight-howard-children/.

141 Moriello, John. "You Won't Believe How Many Kids Pro Bowl Running Back Travis Henry Has Fathered." Sportscasting, May 22, 2020. https://www.sportscasting.com/you-wont-believe-how-many-kids-pro-bowl-running-back-travis-henry-has-fathered/.

142 Rivas, Aby. "Antonio Cromartie Has 14 Children — A Glimpse into the Former NFL Star's Fatherhood." AmoMama, June 26, 2020. https://news.amomama.com/215022-antonio-cromartie-has-14-children-a-glim.html.

143 Tucker, Justin, prod. *The Cromarties* Season 1, Episodes 1-16. Aired November 9, 2017-July 17, 2018 on USA.

144 "Blake Griffin's Only Paying $32K per Month in Child Support." TMZ Sports. TMZ, September 3, 2018. https://www.tmz.com/2018/08/03/blake-griffin-32k-child-support/.

145 Ireland, Sophie. "The World's Wealthiest People (July 18, 2022)." CEOWORLD magazine, July 18, 2022. https://ceoworld.biz/2022/07/18/the-worlds-wealthiest-people-july-18-2022.

146 Grace, Asia. "Elon Musk's next Baby Mama: Hotties Are Applying for the Job." New York Post, July 8, 2022. https://nypost.com/2022/07/08/elon-musks-next-baby-mama-hotties-are-applying-for-the-job/.

147 Musk, Elon (@elonmusk). 2022. "Doing my best to help the underpopulation crisis. A collapsing birth rate is the biggest danger civilization faces by far." Twitter, July 7, 2022, 10:04 a.m. https://twitter.com/elonmusk/status/1545046146548019201?lang=en.

148 Lino, Mark. "The Cost of Raising a Child." U.S. Department of Agriculture, January 13, 2017. https://www.usda.gov/media/blog/2017/01/13/cost-raising-child.

149 Pandolfi, Joseph. "Establishing and Calculating Child Support." Nolo. Accessed April 2, 2023. https://www.nolo.com/legal-encyclopedia/establishing-calculating-child-support-faq.html.

150 "Financial Infidelity: Leading to Divorce." Slater + Gordon, September 14, 2015.

https://www.slatergordon.co.uk/newsroom/financial-infidelity-lies-money-leading-divorce/.

[151] Dr. Phil. "Charles Barkley—What He REALLY Meant By "I Am Not A Role Model."" Youtube video, 05:43. March 25, 2019. https://www.youtube.com/watch?v=IhSqVGYrvhY.

[152] Hawkins, Andrew. "Alvin Kamara." Produced by JPMorgan Chase. *Kneading Dough: The Podcast.* April 1, 2021. Podcast, Apple Podcasts, 01:40:00. https://podcasts.apple.com/us/podcast/alvin-kamara/id1451871735?i=1000515308741.

[153] Hawkins, Andrew. "Alvin Kamara." Produced by JPMorgan Chase. *Kneading Dough: The Podcast.* April 1, 2021. Podcast, Apple Podcasts, 01:40:00. https://podcasts.apple.com/us/podcast/alvin-kamara/id1451871735?i=1000515308741.

[154] Housel, Morgan. *The Psychology of Money: Timeless Lessons on Wealth, Greed, and Happiness.* Petersfield, UK: Harriman House, 2020.

[155] Staff. "Tim Duncan Settles Lawsuit Against Ex-Financial Adviser." NBA.com, January 25, 2018. https://www.nba.com/news/tim-duncan-settles-lawsuit-against-ex-financial-adviser.

[156] Lee, Amber. "25 Athletes Who Got Totally Ripped Off." Bleacher Report, April 5, 2013. https://bleacherreport.com/articles/1593378-25-athletes-who-got-totally-ripped-off.

[157] Dubin, Jared. "Mark Sanchez among Those Defrauded by Investment Advisor's Ponzi-Like Scheme." CBS Sports, June 22, 2016. https://www.cbssports.com/nfl/news/mark-sanchez-among-those-defrauded-by-investment-advisors-ponzi-like-scheme/.

[158] ESPN Films. "30 For 30: Broke." YouTube Video, Released October 6, 2009 https://youtu.be/ib-0_N9G0Lo.

[159] Florio, Mike. "John Elway, Business Partner Lost $15 Million in Ponzi Scheme." NBC Sports, October 14, 2010. https://profootballtalk.nbcsports.com/2010/10/14/john-elway-business-partner-lost-15-million-in-ponzi-scheme.

[160] Staff. "Tyson Sues King For $100 Million." CBS News, March 5, 1998. https://www.cbsnews.com/news/tyson-sues-king-for-100-million.

[161] Reuters. "Ex-NBA Star Garnett Sues Ex-Accountant for $77 Million." Reuters, September 6, 2018. https://www.reuters.com/article/us-basketball-nba-min-garnett-accountant/ex-nba-star-garnett-sues-ex-accountant-for-77-million-idUSKCN1LN079.

[162] West, Jenna. "How Dennis Rodman Discovered He Was Scammed by an Athlete Financial Advisor." Sports Illustrated, September 19, 2019. https://www.si.com/nba/2019/09/19/dennis-rodman-peggy-scammed-financial-advisor.

[163] Jama, Liban. "How Can Athletes Fight the Growing Risk of Being Targeted by Fraud." EY, March 3, 2021. https://www.ey.com/en_us/forensic-integrity-services/how-can-athletes-fight-the-growing-risk-of-being-targeted-by-fraud.

"Article: 6 Steps to Take after Discovering Fraud." Commodity Futures Trading Commission. Accessed April 2, 2023. https://www.cftc.gov/LearnAndProtect/AdvisoriesAndArticles/6Steps.html.

[165] Gronkowski, Rob "Gronk" and Jason Rosenhaus. *It's Good to Be Gronk.* New York, NY: Gallery Books/Jeter Publishing, 2017.

[166] Scipioni, Jade. "Why Rob Gronkowski Wanted to Save All His NFL Paychecks." CNBC, January 30, 2020. https://www.cnbc.com/2020/01/31/why-rob-gronkowski-wanted-to-save-all-his-nfl-paychecks.html.

[167] Williams, Serena, and Rob Haskell. "Serena Williams's Farewell to Tennis-in Her Own Words." Vogue, August 9, 2022. https://www.vogue.com/article/serena-williams-retirement-in-her-own-words.

[168] Williams, Serena, and Rob Haskell. "Serena Williams's Farewell to Tennis-in Her Own Words." Vogue, August 9, 2022. https://www.vogue.com/article/serena-williams-retirement-in-her-own-words.

[169] Verma, Gaurav. "Legendary Golfer Greg Norman Was Forced to Spend an Exorbitant $103 Million to Get Together with Chris Evert." EssentiallySports, August 24, 2022. https://www.essentiallysports.com/wta-tennis-news-legendary-golfer-greg-norman-was-forced-to-spend-an-exorbitant-103-million-to-get-together-with-chris-evert/.

[170] Howard, Caroline, and Kristi Hedges. "Elin Nordegren Walks with $100 Million." ForbesWomen. Forbes, July 3, 2010. https://www.forbes.com/sites/work-in-progress/2010/07/03/elin-nordegren-tiger-woods-divorce-settlement-100-million/?sh=5e0f02951946.

[171] Cardiga, Manuela. "Juanita Vanoy and Michael Jordan's Divorce Cost Him $168 Million — inside Their Split." AmoMama, May 11, 2020. https://news.amomama.com/207619-look-back-juanita-vanoy-michael-jordans.html.

[172] B, Cardi (@iamcardib). 2022. "Why is it far fetch for me to know finance when I have a business ,pay taxes and own stocks ? You gotta know about money to maintain it." Twitter, June 10, 2022, 11:00 a.m. https://twitter.com/iamcardib/status/1535275598754422787?lang=en.

[173] Robbins, Tony. "Why We Do What We Do | TED Talks | Tony Robbins." YouTube video, 23:12. October 1, 2012. https://www.youtube.com/watch?v=BwFOwyoH-3g

[174] Mienaltowski, Andrew. "Everyday Problem Solving across the Adult Life Span: Solution Diversity and Efficacy." *Annals of the New York Academy of Sciences* 1235, no. 1 (2011). https://doi.org/10.1111/j.1749-6632.2011.06207.x.

[175] Ferro, Shaunacy. "The Average Age When People Become Millionaires." Mental Floss, July 14, 2018. https://www.mentalfloss.com/article/550886/average-age-when-people-become-millionaires.

[176] "How Allen Iverson Blew through $200 Million, but Was Saved by a Secret Clause." ClutchPoints, September 10, 2021.

https://clutchpoints.com/how-allen-iverson-blew-through-200-million-but-was-saved-by-a-secret-clause.

177 Carlson, Kyle, Joshua Kim, Annamaria Lusardi, and Colin Camerer. "Bankruptcy Rates among NFL Players with Short-Lived Income Spikes." *American Economic Review* 105, no. 5 (May 2015). https://doi.org/10.3386/w21085.

178 Altman-Devilbiss, Alexx. "Sc Becomes 15th State to Require Personal Finance Course for High School Graduates." WPDE. ABC, July 9, 2022. https://wpde.com/news/local/south-carolina-becomes-15th-state-to-require-personal-finance-course-for-high-school-graduates.

179 Greenspan, Alan and Board of Governors of the Federal Reserve System. *Statement on Financial Literacy.* Addressed to the Committee on Banking, Housing, and Urban Affairs, United States Senate. February 5, 2002. https://fraser.stlouisfed.org/title/statements-speeches-alan-greenspan-452/financial-literacy-8754/fulltext

180 Lin, Judy T. Bumcrot, Christopher. Mottola, Gary. Valdes, Olivia. Ganem, Robert. Kieffer, Christine. Walsh, Gerri. *Financial Capability in the United States.* ed. 5. Wilmington, DE: FINRA Investor Education Foundation, 2022. https://finrafoundation.org/sites/finrafoundation/files/NFCS-Report-Fifth-Edition-July-2022.pdf.

181 "Homepage." National Football League Players Association. Accessed April 3, 2023. https://nflpa.com/.

"Homepage." National Basketball Players Association. Accessed April 3, 2023. https://nbpa.com/.

"Homepage." Womens' National Basketball Players Association. Accessed April 3, 2023. https://wnbpa.com/.

"Homepage." Major League Baseball Players. Accessed April 3, 2023. https://www.mlbplayers.com/.

"Homepage." National Hockey League Players Association. Accessed April 3, 2023. https://www.nhlpa.com/.

"Homepage." Major League Sports Players Association. Accessed April 3, 2023. https://mlsplayers.org/.

182 "About #AthleteAnd." National Football League Players Association. #AthleteAnd Podcast. Accessed April 3, 2023. https://nflpa.com/athleteand.

183 "About #AthleteAnd." National Football League Players Association. #AthleteAnd Podcast. Accessed April 3, 2023. https://nflpa.com/athleteand.

184 Santamaria, Carlos, and Ari Winkleman. "The Graphic Truth: Racial Diversity in US Professional Sports." GZERO Media, August 31, 2020. https://www.gzeromedia.com/the-graphic-truth-racial-diversity-in-us-professional-sports.

[185] "Finance Advisor Demographics and Statistics [2023]: Number of Finance Advisors in the US." Zippia. Accessed April 3, 2023. https://www.zippia.com/finance-advisor-jobs/demographics/.

[186] Raimonde, Olivia. "There Are More than 600,000 Millennial Millionaires in the US, According to Report." CNBC, October 16, 2019. https://www.cnbc.com/amp/2019/10/16/us-has-more-than-600000-millennial-millionaires-according-to-report.html.

[187] PYMNTS. *Reality Check: The Paycheck-to-Paycheck Report December 2021.* San Francisco, CA: LendingClub, 2021. https://www.pymnts.com/study/reality-check-paycheck-to-paycheck-pandemic-inflation-rising-costs/.

[188] Hosick, Michelle Brutlag. "NCAA Adopts Interim Name, Image and Likeness Policy." NCAA, December 30, 2021. https://www.ncaa.org/news/2021/6/30/ncaa-adopts-interim-name-image-and-likeness-policy.aspx.

ABOUT THE AUTHOR

Lynda Paul is the owner, founder, and chief investment advisor of Sound Money Management, Inc., RIA, an independent Registered Investment Advisory firm in San Antonio, Texas. She is a Certified Financial Planner® professional and an inactive CPA. With an undergraduate degree in corporate finance from Ball State University and a master's degree in finance / accounting and marketing from Keller Graduate School of Management, Lynda is celebrating 28 years serving the needs of her clients in a spectacular way, operating her firm as a fiduciary. Lynda believes that when it comes to choosing a financial planner, independence, trust, and competence are foundational virtues. She has helped more than 500 clients achieve their financial goals and manages millions of dollars for her clients around the country.

Over the past decades, Lynda has served several organizations in the Chicagoland area with passion and honor, including being a fundraiser for Red Nose Day, to help spread awareness and to end the cycle of child poverty, Roots & Wings, a young men's ministry she founded in 2001, creating the Jabez Project, Chair of the Finance Committee for the YWCA Board of Directors, and from 2011 to 2017, as an elected member of the College of Lake County Board of Trustees. Lynda founded the Illinois Hoopstars AAU Boys Basketball Program in 2001 and tallied a 97% win ratio during her years of coaching.

As a former Division I collegiate basketball player, Lynda has combined her passions for financial planning and athletic endeavors to create an inspiring and informative book about the importance of financial literacy titled *Making Sound Money Moves: Financial Playbook for All Jocks – 43 Reasons Professional Athletes Have Jacked-Up Financial Lives and What You Can Learn from Their Foul Plays*. Her goal for this book is "to inspire young people to improve their financial IQ and relationship with money, and to help them understand that money decisions made today will impact their future."

Lynda is married to Cliffton Paul, Sr., a retired police officer and Navy veteran, and they have three wonderful Millennial sons: Cliff Jr., Brandon, and Darius. In her leisure time, Lynda enjoys hiking, whitewater rafting, teaching Zumba and cardio-kickboxing, and reading up on financial planning strategies while hanging out at the beach.

Lynda speaks to audiences around the country on various topics on financial literacy, financial planning, and leaving a financial legacy.

Follow Lynda: **LyndaPaul.com**

Book Lynda to Speak: LyndaPaul.com/speaking

Get added to the waitlist for the next Sound Money MasterClass LyndaPaul.com/courses

Lynda's life goal: "Skate where the puck will be," a twist on Wayne Gretzky's famous quote

Favorite word: peripeteia

Favorite emotion: delicious

Ideal brunch date: Mellody L. Hobson, downtown Chicago

Ideal pre-dinner date: having a refreshing beverage with Megan Thee Stallion in H-Town

Ideal dinner date: Brooke Castillo (The LCS) in Miami

Mellody, Megan, and Brooke, future Girls' Trip?

Lynda Paul

It's *Go* Time!
Everyone has a role to play.

Together we can improve our financial literacy,
one sound money move at a time.

Photo Credit: Richard's Photography, San Antonio, Texas

What will be your financial legacy?

Author: Lynda Paul, CFP, CPA, MBA
The Money Coach
LyndaPaul.com

Copies of this book can be purchased from Amazon or LyndaPaul.com

Live Events, Webinars, MasterClass, and Private Workshops: LyndaPaul.com/events

Book Signing Locations: LyndaPaul.com/events

Purchase Cool Gear and Piggy Banks: LyndaPaul.com/store

Speaking Engagements: LyndaPaul.com/speaking

Group Coaching (Topic Specific): LyndaPaul.com/courses

Hire Lynda for personal financial planning: LyndaPaul.com/coaching or SoundMoneySanAntonio.com

Her firm's Form ADV is available upon request.

If you enjoyed reading this book and found it to be a valuable resource, please add a book review at Amazon.com today. Every review is read to see what you thought about the content and your book review will help new readers discover this book. **Thank you!**

Printed in the USA
CPSIA information can be obtained
at www.ICGtesting.com
CBHW051237311023
1598CB00003B/7